The Sales Assassin
Master Your Black Belt in Sales

Anthony Caliendo

TIGER SHARK
MEDIA USA

Anthony Caliendo

Author, Speaker, Entrepreneur and Leadership Coach

Sandra Kanies-Caliendo

Dedicated to a Woman of Strength and Sacrifice

DEDICATION

"The bond between mothers and their children is one defined by love. As a mother's prayers for her children are unending, so are the wisdom, grace, and strength they provide to their children."
—George W. Bush

My mother, Sandra Kanies-Caliendo, is the essence of hard work. She is and will always be a source of strength and a rock and foundation in my life. I dedicate this book to her because of my respect for a woman who never gave up and instilled discipline in her children. She was the one who had direct influence on my drive and my desire to be an excellent provider and good father to my children. Life was not easy for a woman who raised three children on her own. She has never allowed me to succumb to failure for she instilled in us undying fortitude. It was this fortitude that allowed her to become one of the top pharmaceutical sales people for Squibb during a time when it was more difficult for women to succeed in business. Her success in the male dominated world was due to understanding the sacrifices she had to make in order to support the family and to succeed in her business life. We knew that her sacrifices came from the love that she had for her children and I want her to know that she did an incredible job setting the right example.

Mom, I'm proud of you and because of you I am able to stand

proud of who I am and what I desire to be. You have been a great example and a source of strength and your example has enabled me to grow and be stronger. We have never been a family that expressed our love for one another through flowery words. But our love for one another was expressed through our faith and commitment to each other. I have grown and become my own person. Your example taught me to nourish my own family through the love carried in my heart. I understand the sacrifices that you made in order to support the family and through you I gained a sense of responsibility and desire to succeed from watching you each day. I know your sacrifices came from the love that you had for your children and I want you to know that you did an incredible job and I'm proud of you.

THE BEGINNING
FROM LEMONADE
TO THE SALES ASSASSIN

My lemonade was nothing more than another word for money. Lemonade was not in my blood. It wasn't those big juicy lemons that made my cheeks pucker and it wasn't the sugar that gave me that sweet tang in my mouth. It wasn't the Crayola colorful signs I made with my broken crayons and it wasn't the ice that made this simple drink perfect on a summer day. It was a passionate desire to earn money that pumped my blood. Money was perfection. Perfection was the chase—the chase for every car, the chase for every person that walked by my house. Lemonade was nothing more than a means to success. But making money ran through my veins by the time I was eight. Sales became my passion. I loved the excitement. I loved the anticipation. I loved the hunt, the chase. I loved the precision of the hunt. I loved finding the target. I loved the success. My prey was not to be destroyed, but to be drawn to me and me to them. At that point, I could smell success—the close. It was at that moment, from a Lemonade Stand, that I became "The Sales Assassin.

Anthony Caliendo
The Ultimate Sales Assassin Master

ACKNOWLEDGEMENTS

Lynette DeBiase-Caliendo—My wife, mother of my children, life partner—Thank you for being simply you. Your love and faith in me mean so much. How you put up with me and all my idiosyncrasies makes me smile each day and know how blessed I am to have you as the cornerstone of my life. You are always there for me and our kids. You keep our world and family forever strong. You know that I am a man of few words, but this is an occasion when I want to say how much you mean to me and thank you for your strength, support and patience.

***

Master Instructor Joe Goytia, Goytia's Martial Arts—When I was a young manager at Chicago Health Clubs, Joe was teaching Jeet Kune Do, Kali and Silat in one of the upstairs studios and I would go up and train with him and his students. I was eager to learn. Joe's skill level was impressive, having achieved Black Belts in Tae Kwan Do, Hapkido, and Karate and achieved his instructorship in Jeet Kune Do. Recognizing each other's talents and strengths, we went into business together in 1990 and opened The Asian Fighting Arts Academy on 63rd and California, one of the roughest areas of Chicago. Later in life, we've both come to realize how impactful this experience was for both of us. Joe once told me that had it not been for my sales, marketing and business know-how, he would have never realized that one cannot operate and sustain a successful business on technical skill alone. Likewise, all of the tactical and philosophical principles of the martial arts that I know, I learned from Joe, while observing and feeding off his crazy energy and enthusiasm for the art. And I realized as I began writing and structuring "The Sales Assassin," that these principles influence me to this very day. Today we both live by the creed that having pure, unadulterated mental and physical discipline, as well as having an unambiguous set of tactics and philosophies, is key to achieving success in business and in life.

Ronald Moskovsky (deceased *12/4/12*). Ron was my Area Supervisor at Chicago Health Clubs and was the person who gave me my very first management opportunity. This was my very first role where I had to learn how to build and motivate a sales team. I excelled at it and learned that I possessed an innate skill set that would be the basis for my career goals. Ron recognized this about me, perhaps, even before I realized it about myself. He was and always will be an inspiration. May he rest in peace.

Al Philips and Margaret Ceja—Al Philips is legendary in the health club business, owning several World Gyms in the Chicago, Indiana and Wisconsin regions. When he left Bally's back in the early 90s to build the World Gyms with Arnold Schwarzenegger, he selected me to help build his dream. He became my mentor, my motivator and brought out the best in me relating to work ethic and drive. Margaret Ceja, current founder and President/CEO of Ideal Fitness Solutions, worked with Al and she was the one who exposed me to the operational side of the business. She helped me realize that in order to be successful at any business, the operations and management can be just as "make or break" as the sales side. I appreciate them both for influencing my early beginnings in sales and in business as a whole.

David Aguilera, Edward Oski and John "TJ" Kim, Jr.—my Chicago homeboys whom I am proud to call friends to this day. David, Edward and I were in the health club business together back in Chicago. David was actually my opposite in that he was conservative and restrained in his approach to life and business whereas I was aggressive and impulsive. However, he was a true friend, talented and intelligent, that helped me find that balance later on in life. Edward was my former roommate, "aces" and partners in business since we were 18 years old. No matter what our stations in life have been, Ed has remained one of my most loyal friends and confidants. John Kim, otherwise known as "TJ (Table Jockey)" and I worked together as young stockbrokers. We were friendly rivals who pushed one another to be the top in sales. We were both with the same firm when we moved to South Florida and have been business associates and close friends ever since. These three gentlemen taught me that true friendship is invaluable.

Enrique "Rick" Rodriguez—Rick and I also worked together as stockbrokers and have been close business associates throughout the years. But we've also become close friends and family men, traveling together and raising our children together alongside our wives. We've relied on one another personally and professionally and our children are growing up together becoming the best of friends as well. I can say unequivocally that he's one of the best producers, best fathers and best husbands I know. I admire him and value his camaraderie.

Mary Beth Tomasino—Mary Beth is the President/CEO of JVM

Sales Corp d/b/a Milano's Cheese, our Italian cheese manufacturing plant in NJ. Observing her passion and spirit for the business she loves, has been an awe-inspiring thing. After I left the mortgage business, I was introduced to the Italian cheese business and the JVM Sales operation. What I saw was a "diamond in the rough" and an incredible opportunity to help lead the organization to be recognized as the #1 Italian cheese company in the US. Our visions were in sync. Mary Beth is a powerhouse woman in business with a relentless work ethic that inspired me to tackle and conquer the Italian cheese industry head on. She is a lady that I respect and admire.

Daniel Kodsi—Dan is the President/CEO of RPC Holdings and luxury real estate developer and mogul in South Florida. At a time in my life when I needed someone to believe in me, Dan was there. He was the type of business partner and friend who did things for me without hesitation because of his belief in me. I admired his achievements in the real estate game and it was Dan whom I strived to emulate when I decided to pursue mortgage and real estate. What a class act.

Lead Me Media and Rob Clouse—My official Internet marketing partner whose investment and commitment to the exposure and promotion of this project has been invaluable. Rob is truly one of the most talented and resourceful men in the Internet marketing business! I welcome him to the team and look forward to reveling in our success.

Marv Russell—My editor, project coordinator and fellow cigar aficionado whom I met at precisely the right place and the right time in my life. Thanks to Marv's insight, expertise and for keeping us on track throughout this journey of bringing "The Sales Assassin" to life.

Rickey Greene, Rickey Greene Designs—The most gifted and brilliant graphic artist and marketing designer in the business, who never ceases to stun and amaze us with his talents. Being able to entrust someone implicitly with visually capturing your ideas is so invaluable when sales, marketing and image is so very important to your livelihood. Rickey is that someone, and has been such an integral part of my marketing team for over 10 years. Without his creative eye and aesthetic talents, there would be no "sizzle to the steak!"

Jonathan Vinazza aka "Johnny Web," Underlab Studios—An eccentric and insanely smart and talented artist; a master in design, development, branding and image who brings invaluable technical social networking, video marketing and media production expertise to the project. We call him "Johnny Web." He's always viewed the world through a different pair of glasses and I've enjoyed watching him mature in depth and in knowledge over the past 11 years. When I propositioned him with "The Sales Assassin" project, he only impressed me more with his immense aptitude and understanding of today's marketing standards. He's a main ingredient and I'm grateful for his commitment to the team.

Catherine Russell, HireCatherine LLC—Thanks to Catherine, a welcomed addition to our team, whose social media marketing skills and savvy has helped catapult our project in a very important and necessary way. You've captured the spirit of The Sales Assassin effortlessly and brilliantly.

Philip and Angela Caliendo—My siblings whom I love and

respect. As children, we all observed my mother make incredible sacrifices just to support us. We relied upon each other to make our house a home. I am truly proud of the man, woman, father and mother that they've become. We may have lived by different creeds or have had different approaches to life, but I admire and respect them both for being responsible, standing on their own and becoming loving support systems for their families.

Phil Caliendo—To my father, who passed away when I was writing "The Sales Assassin." I thank him for the gift of life, for his lessons in life, and for inspiring me to be the best father that I can be to my children. May he rest in peace.

***

Krystal Harvey—Business Manager and partner—the word partner means so many things—collaborator, associate, coworker, confidant, advisor and more. Krystal and I have partnered for 11 years in every business venture imaginable. I have valued her contribution to the success of my business. She has demonstrated great imagination, vision and business savvy and is a Sales Assassin in every sense of the word. She is a trusted colleague and integral member of my business team. We have been able to learn from one another and challenge each other to be our best. Thank you for your insights and contributions to this book. Without your hard work, this book would not have been possible.

THE MEN AND WOMEN OF THE UNITED STATES ARMED FORCES

I'd like to acknowledge this courageous and valiant breed of individuals who serve and protect this great Nation of ours. Thank you for what you stand for and for fighting for our freedoms that so many of us take for granted. I hold you in the highest regard and salute you each and every day.

TABLE OF CONTENTS

PROLOGUE

THE SALES ASSASSIN is the ultimate master of sales passion and discipline, the *Sales Assassin Master* (aka SAM) of your own destiny, focused on a results-driven willingness to be prepared to control your own destiny. A SAM must be an entrepreneur of their life and business no matter what name is on your title. The SAM begins with a foundation of individual discipline built on a positive attitude and reinforced through your personal and moral commitment to sales success. A SAM is focused on everything positive in a sales person's life from family to a sales person as an individual to customers and clients. The SAM must be a master of perseverance, self-control and must possess the spirit of being responsible and accountable for your successful performance. The organization must be charged with developing and supporting the SAM mentality and tools and techniques required for success. It takes hard work to achieve SAM status. This book describes the path to Sales Assassin success—the path to positive thinking—the path to controlling your sales destiny as a SAM and the company's understanding of how SAM benefits the organization's sales strategy and corporate success.

> *"Failure is the condiment that gives success its flavor."*[1]
> —Truman Capote

It is my goal to mold and shape the way you think and act and the way the corporation develops the SAM mentality in its' sales forces—to pass on to you and the corporation how and why I have

---

1   http://www.pbs.org/wnet/americanmasters/episodes/truman-capote/introduction/58/

become known as the *Ultimate Sales Assassin Master*. Salesmanship is not easy. I have had successes and failures throughout my life. I like most people have failed at different times in my life, but I have never known nor will I yield to defeat. I have taught sales people and corporations throughout my professional life. I have shared my successes and failures and I have shared how I was challenged and allowed to rise to higher, more effective performance levels. I have learned and taught others that a SAM will not be defeated, but will persevere when the odds are against you, when the economy is tough, when the competition appears bigger and stronger. In these cases, my mastery is a dominant force that will not yield to defeat. It is my precision and passion and your precision and passion that lead to Sales Assassin Mastery.

> *"Remember that failure is an event—not a person."*[2]
> —Zig Ziglar

Ice to Eskimos

When I was young, my family was in the Italian food business and one of our main products was Italian ice. One day, my Father and my Uncle told me that we had just sold truckloads of Italian ice to an establishment in Alaska. They poignantly told me "Son, one day you're going to be the very best salesman there is. Your family just sold ice to Eskimos!" Even though by that time my desire for success and making money was already there, I think perhaps those words planted a deeper seed inside of me. Perhaps those words validated me and they made me feel invincible and proud of my name. Today, I still carry them around with me like a badge of honor and I share the "Ice to Eskimos" story with all of my sales people as a source of inspiration. It's also become a directive and my

---

2   http://www.ziglar.com

mantra to achieve the impossible. "Go out and sell Ice to Eskimos" means dare to achieve the impossible.

The fact that you're reading this book is proof that you've already accepted the need to improve and challenge yourself to become an exceptional sales professional. The fact that you bought this book tells me that you've bought others, attended sales seminars, watched videos and listened to tapes. I'm willing to bet that most career salespeople reading this book have spent hundreds of dollars on these types of tools, hoping to take away with them the skills and hopefully the magic formula needed to become a better salesperson. Now ask yourself and be honest, what has been your ROI? Dollars to doughnuts, you're still trying to cash in on those other tools. If you want to achieve SAM status then you must be willing to make a bigger investment and accept a certain amount of risk. I guarantee you that "The Sales Assassin" is the book that will give you the right tools to earn your Return On Investment (ROI).

INTRODUCTION

"Enchantment is the purest form of sales. <u>Enchantment</u> is all about changing people's hearts, minds and actions because you provide them a vision or a way to do things better. The difference between enchantment and simple sales is that with enchantment you have the other person's best interests at heart, too."[3]

—Guy Kawasaki

Author, Venture Capitalist and Technologist and former Chief Evangelist at Apple Computer

The Ultimate Sales Assassin Master at Work

When I stop by Starbucks for my early morning coffee, I shake my head at the number of sales people sitting at tables sorting through paper, scrolling through their iPhones and wildly navigating on their tablets—on the phone, off the phone—shaking their head in defeat. What the hell are they doing? Never does a day go by when I'm not asked by sales people, "Hey aren't you *The Main Man*?" How can I be more successful in sales?" or "How can I become a Sales Assassin?"

There's probably not a sales book I haven't read and there is probably not a sales book that doesn't have some value, but yet there isn't one that I finish saying, "wow, that was great." You see my problem is that these books come from the same starting point: A sale is the exchange of money for a product or service that results from an interaction. The process is your ability to engage a prospect on

---

3   Kawasaki, G., http://www.amazon.com/Enchantment-Changing-Hearts-Minds-Actions/
     dp/1591845831/ref=sr_1_1?ie=UTF8&qid=1387470545&sr=8-1&keywords=GUY+KAWASAKI

a personal level. My starting point begins with discovery of your SAM Distinctive Nature to Achieve—Your SAM DNA. Your SAM DNA is your ability to achieve success while overcoming failure. The SAM will find success through his or her passion, dedication and courage to overcome the great challenges of the toughest market place and the toughest competition. Through this book you must find and define your SAM DNA.

> *"Salespeople today ARE the differentiator. That's why it's so critical for you to focus on becoming a valuable business asset to your customers."*[4]
> —Jill Konrath
>
> Author of *"SNAP Selling"* and *"Selling to BIG Companies"*

The Main Man

I read an article written about me a few years back where the author described me as a "marketing machine." In those days I was known across the southeastern US as "The Main Man—A Marketing Machine." I am an entrepreneur with exceptional instincts of salesmanship. I guess I won't disagree with the statement of being a marketing machine, but I'm so much more and this book is so much more than the lessons of a marketing machine. Better stated, I am an Entrepreneurial Machine and this book describes the mechanical and instinctive skills that you must practice, demonstrate and refine for success. These are the lessons of the "Ultimate Sale Assassin Master." I am a Samurai—a sheaf of glistening sales skills that does not cut, but systematically carves my way to sales success. For over 25 years I have been molded by self-discovering the art and mastery of drawing customers to me and delivering products and service through superior

---

4   Konrath, J., http://www.jillkonrath.com.

performance. Anthony Caliendo's sales mastery is the result of the successes and failures in my life. The successes in my life are not the result of doing all the right things, but instead they result from being willing to fail in a way that enables me to continuously learn how to succeed. The tools of this samurai have come from the passion for sales that I found in my body, mind and spirit. My spirit is the tenacity you can achieve growing up without a father on the Southside of Chicago. I found my instincts for survival on the streets, a place where a lack of discipline can quickly take your mind to ridiculously bad decisions and where your body must be strong enough to defeat those who desire to take life from you in any way possible.

My father was not there, but his legacy hung over my head, reminding me that a family name would not define me, but would instead free me to pursue what was not always the right direction, but it was my direction.

***

Wisdom from Anthony Caliendo, the Ultimate Sales Assassin

In overcoming life's adversity and the difficult circumstances we will face in life, it is your ability to learn from the past and recreate yourself for today and the future.

Not many 18 year olds today would have the guts or be given the respect and trust to lead the development and management of an operation such as Chicago Health Clubs. In those days, I had no fear. Six years later, at age 24, I only had success and money on my mind and that led the SVP of this great club to ask me to help build World Gyms with Arnold Schwarzenegger. This was not a career. This was excitement. I felt no stress. I felt no anxiety. But even with Mr. Universe as a business colleague, I was not satisfied. Sure, working with Arnold was very cool and I became the envy of my Southside running buddies. We all loved the White Sox. We all hated the Cubs and as for the Chicago Bears, all I can say is I too became one of the "Monsters of Midway." When I left World Gym, I headed across the street to the Chicago Stock Exchange. Anyone who has worked in this world whether in Chicago or on Wall Street knows the idea of survival of the fittest. Let's put it this way: In those days, any NFL offensive player's blood ran cold when stared down by the likes of Bears linebacker Mike Singletary. My eyes, my heart, my spirit, my willingness to sacrifice were no less than that of Iron Mike Singletary. By the time the mid-1990s hit I was one of the most successful brokers when the market boomed.

But how far can a stockbroker go with just great instincts and passion, but only barely surviving high school? I realized that change had to be in the cards for me. Accepting, managing and growing through change were core to me. As I put the pieces of the Anthony Caliendo philosophy of sales together for this book, it forced me to take stock of every business that I had engaged in that led to this moment.

The beginning of my sales journey was the pennies, nickels and dimes I earned from childhood activities. Each one of these efforts was a learning opportunity and this learning was core to my growth and evolution to becoming the Ultimate Sales Assassin. Learning is a life-long phenomenon. It is not always organized or compartmentalized to the classroom. It will not always be seen or felt, but instead it will likely be absorbed and combined with other experiences—building to something greater as we get older and mature. This is me. What I have learned in this world and especially what I have learned about sales has been an evolution. My evolution has resulted from my love and passion for what I do.

My love for what I was doing was immense. However, a new life and new business opportunities awaited me in South Florida. This change would be a cornerstone in my career. The prosperous world of mortgage financing was changing life for many during the South Florida real estate boom of the new millennium. I wanted my share of the American Apple Pie. By 2005, my new company had grossed over $83 million in loan volume. I became "The Main Man;" radio, television and newspapers featured the mortgage world's version of "Rocky, The Italian Stallion." I wasn't the underdog by any means, but my life forced me to take a lot of punches, but I could dish it out with precision. My company became the official mortgage company to the Miami Heat, the Dolphins and Florida Marlins radio networks. In fact, one day I bumped into Dan Marino, the great QB of the Dolphins, "Hey you're The Main Man!" We shook hands as he reminded me smiling, "But I'm Dan the Man."

The "Main Man" with Dan "The Man" Marino

"El Hombre Principal" with my Coral Gables staff at our Mortgage Company Holiday Yacht Party, 2004

My success in the mortgage and real estate world was tough work even in the best economy. The hard work paid off in so many ways, but the best of the Sales Assassins took huge hits in 2007 when the economy and real estate tanked. I was among the ones who took a severe blow to the jaw. I was one who lived on the edge. For The Main Man, I had put it all on the line. In those moments, most people would see no place else to go but down. Not me. Another opportunity was waiting, reinventing myself, creating a new Anthony Caliendo, creating a new brand. As the Ultimate Sales Assassin Master, I would live to fight and rise to the top again.

My rebranding would lead to a new partnership as the national sales and marketing leader with a 25-year-old cheese manufacturing company. There was some trepidation. But because of the SAM I am, I was able to confront those emotions head on. My business manager, Krystal Harvey, described me as "fearless." Yes, I am fearless and today, I'm the "Big Cheese", aka "The Cheese Boss" at 1-800-BIG-Cheese. I am one of the largest Italian cheese salesmen in the U.S.

Milano's Cheese at the 2013 International Pizza Expo,
Las Vegas with Justin Tomasino

For a SAM there is no place else to go but forward and back to the top. With my tenacious sales mentality, I've been able to generate over $60 million in revenue for the company within 5 years. Currently, my sales office is generating over $20 million in sales annually and rapidly growing. The Sales Assassin has nowhere to go except forward.

Wisdom from Anthony Caliendo, the Ultimate Sales Assassin

The Sales Assassin's Success is knowing your strengths, recognizing your limitations and then moving on to new challenges, new mastery and new opportunities.

The Philosophy and Structure of The Sales Assassin

I've trained thousands of sales professionals and top producers across numerous industries. My chief strategy to helping my sales people succeed in sales has always been in getting them to focus on identifying and overcoming the underlying behaviors that prevent them from meeting their goals. This strategy is universal and transcends any and all other strategies or philosophies aimed at helping sales professionals succeed. My book demands a shift in the philosophy around the sales process that corporations and sales professionals engage each day. The traditional sales philosophy teaches you basic concepts, like getting to work early and being the last to leave will help you improve your work ethic. Or like prioritizing your day to a perfect "T" will help you to become more productive.

My philosophy is a comprehensive sales approach that begins where the other philosophies end. This book is not the concepts that you find in "Sales 101" because the purpose of this book is to expose you to new ideas and tools designed to elevate you from where you are as an ordinary salesperson into Sales Assassin Mastery. This philosophy demands and allows you to redefine yourself providing guidance for self-improvement, not only as a salesperson, but also as an individual. You will achieve this by understanding the key pieces of the puzzle and how and why these pieces are strategically placed together to apply on a daily basis and in every day, real life situations.

I enjoy teaching and through this book I am going to teach you not to just learn how to sell products and services, but also to learn to:

- spend more time gathering the knowledge you need to become a better sales person
- take more time to identify your shortcomings and to adopt the correct mindset to overcome these shortcomings
- mold, shape and help you through the transition process and elevate the average sales person from being the conventional to the exceptional
- see the distinction between the conventional sales philosophy and an exceptional SAM sales philosophy

Traditionally, sales books talk about a sales strategy as a plan that hopefully puts a company and its products in a position to gain a competitive advantage. These strategies supposedly help organizations and you focus on potential customers and communicate with them in a way that is meaningful and results in sales. Traditionally, the idea is that all you need to know is how products or services can solve customer problems. Then all you should have to do is focus on four things:

1. Find and identify potential customers

2. Qualify customers

3. Make a proposal

4. Close the sale

Yes, these four things are valid and it is where traditional sales strategy begins, however each of us has so much more to learn and experience. This book is designed to take you beyond these four traditional elements of life in the sales industry. However, the key question you must ask yourself is once you have learned the distinction and recognize the philosophical superiority of the SAM sales model:

How do you develop the desire to make the changes necessary to adopt the SAM sales model? There are five steps to this process:

1. Figure out if you really like what you do.

2. Determine if you believe in sales as a viable career; or are you in a sales job because you have failed at other careers.

3. Determine if your personality, your life style and your ways of thinking are suited for a career in sales.

4. Determine if you can become passionate about your career each day and especially when the economy is tough.

5. Determine what changes you must make in order to drive your success and determine if these changes will be impactful enough to begin your transformation process. For example,

   a. Does fear need to evolve into courage?

   b. Does complacency need to evolve into drive and persistency?

   c. Do you make excuses?

d. What things about your personality need to be examined and can they (realistically) become modified?

If the changes you need to make are impactful, then that burning flame of desire will stay alive as you observe permanent, beneficial changes being manifested within yourself. Without being able to answer these questions and others and feel good about your responses, it will be almost impossible for you to advance through the belts to becoming a SAM.

***

The Old Sales Mentality

Here's your desk. Here's your phone. Now you're on your own!

Recently I went into a local wireless company in search of a new phone. Two young men were sitting at their facing desks. Another customer was looking at phones just like me. After 5 minutes, I realized neither I nor the other customer had yet to be approached. One of the sales persons was playing with his phone; I assume texting or playing a game and the other seemed to be doing paperwork. **Strike 1**

Different from the other customer, I asked for some help. The texting sales guy lifted his head and said, "How can I help you?" Now understand, with the exception of his head and lips, nothing else moved. The phone was still in his hand and he still did not stand up or introduce himself. **Strike 2**

I said simply that I currently have an iPhone and I was thinking about changing models and would like to know the difference in one model versus another. One would assume at this point this guy is ready to sell me a phone. His response to my question, "Well that depends on your needs." My patience was now running thin, after all I'm a hot-blooded, Italian sales machine. Ok I'll go along for now and responded, "I need a phone that does a good job with email, texting and I can get what I need online." His response, "Well, the phone you have will do that." **Strike 3, You're Out.**

The best sales strategy in the world is worthless without the proper attitude, passion and mentality. This book is not only about the sales process, but also it's about your ability to understand your product and how this product will engage customers. The time you spend in front of your customers is a precious commodity that must be managed properly in terms of what you say, what you do, how you present yourself. No matter if you work for a company or whether you're a business owner, a salesperson must treat the profession as being in business for yourself. Each of these elements is a product of your mentality—The Sales Assassin Mastery Mentality.

I see the sales world as very similar to my martial arts training with Master Instructor Joe Goytia in Jeet Kune Do and Kali Silat. Just like the kid who starts karate lessons has a vision of the movie "The Karate Kid," the major problem with sales people is they perceive sales as the great opportunity to make lots of money. They see the glory not the hard work. Some students succeed and others give up after a few lessons when they realize that the fun comes only after hard work and a lot of sweat. They give up, but will always say *I studied martial arts*. In my experience the sales professional, like the karate student, must commit to develop a number of skills and a very specific mind-set to enable him or her to create success.

I have seen many sales systems and processes just like there are many forms of martial arts. We each swear our system is the best and will reap great rewards. These processes are not that different, but like martial arts, success is the art of mastering certain characteristics that transcend the process regimentation.

This book speaks to corporations and sales professionals who are constantly searching for the formula that will provide you with an edge against the competition. Organizations and sales professionals struggle with understanding if the sales process they are using is the right one that addresses the obstacles they face each day. My theory is the problem sales organizations face is not about the process but rather must place a renewed focus on the training of the sales professional to acquire new sets of skills and a new mentality in using the sales process. In every other function of a company, money is spent developing the competencies of leaders. But these leaders are teaching their functional employees how to achieve success. The sales organization must also invest money and time in developing their sales team.

My years of experience working with corporations and sales professionals have taught me a couple of key points:

1. Sales professionals need a clear, specific, target-based process.

2. Sales professionals must be molded and shaped, but they must also possess sales instincts that avoid chasing nebulous opportunities.

3. Sales professionals will not succeed unless they know and understand who they are and what attitude and personal skill attributes they will need for success. The best sales process will not be successful unless the sales professional

embraces the skills and changes required to overcome the odds and the challenges placed before them.

I have designed this book around *9 Belts of Sales Assassin Mastery*. Each belt is more than a step in the Sales Assassin Mastery process. The belts represent a component of my philosophy and a way of life that supports Sales Assassin Mastery success. Each belt is achieved through mental and physical commitment and sacrifice. The belts in the SAM Sales Philosophy are generally analogous to the martial arts philosophy, as most people would understand. However, the belts are not intended to be progressive, but instead they are a series of elements and skills that exist independent of one another, but collectively provide a professional foundation for sales success. Each belt reflects the SAM's proven level of competence and just as importantly; each reflects an inner sales journey, a journey that never ends, and a step toward continuous improvement. When you understand the importance of each belt and how to embrace the concepts you must achieve to be awarded each belt, this is an accomplishment worthy of respect and one that measures another step toward success.

When I created these 9 Belts and decided what I wanted each belt to represent, I drew from my own experiences with Master Instructor Joe Goytia. Master Goytia first exposed me to the tactical and philosophical principles of martial arts. On some subconscious level, those two principles have absolutely influenced my every day approach to business and life. This revelation became evident to me when I began structuring my sales philosophy around the 9 Belts. When it comes to sales, I believe in physical and mental discipline and commitment and I absolutely believe that the tactical lessons are equally as important as the philosophical.

Tactically in martial arts, one should be able to anticipate his or her opponent's fighting style, his next strike and be able to counter those strikes with an intensely superior assault intending to defeat. In sales, one must be able to use his or her instinct and take calculated risks in order to navigate through the inevitable peaks and valleys. Philosophically, Jeet Kune Do teaches one the principle of continuous evolution and learning to improve by absorbing what is useful and disregarding and replacing what is not. Likewise, in sales, the same principal applies in that you have to consistently take stock in yourself, reinvest, reinvent and learn from successes and failures. You must always have the courage to make the changes necessary to excel to the next level.

***

> *"If you always put limits on everything you do, physical or anything else, it will spread into your work and into your life. There are no limits. There are only plateaus, and you must not stay there, you must go beyond them."*[5]
> —Bruce Lee

Don't worry, I don't expect you to become the next Bruce Lee, but he is very correct. You can't put limits on everything you do. My 9 belts of the SAM process, in the same way as the great Master of Jeet Kune Do, remove your limits and provide invaluable tactical and philosophical knowledge, skills and abilities that will differentiate you from your competition.

- ❖ SAM Belt 1: Passion, Dedication, Courage
- ❖ SAM Belt 2: Mental Preparedness Development
- ❖ SAM Belt 3: Establishing the Sales Assassin Mindset

5   Goodreads. https://www.goodreads.com/author/quotes/32579.Bruce_Lee

- ❖ SAM Belt 4: Goal Setting and Achievement
- ❖ SAM Belt 5: Client Qualification Process
- ❖ SAM Belt 6: The Mastery of Leadership Integrity
- ❖ SAM Belt 7: Reinvestment in Your Business and You
- ❖ SAM Belt 8: Lessons of Life
- ❖ SAM Belt 9: Lifestyle Change

Each SAM element will end with a summary advice called *Wisdoms from the Ultimate Sales Assassin Master*. This book will also include a number of exercises to assist my SAM students in developing their personal commitment to the *Pathway to SAM Excellence*.

9 Belts of the Sales Assassin

***

Finally, you might be approaching this book from a sales professional perspective, or from a personal point of view. Perhaps you are looking to learn how to manage and negotiate adversity, persevere against the odds and contribute to your own professional success or to the professional success of your team around you. Maybe you are reading this book as a member or leader of a professional association.

You might view this book from the perspective of a leader of a multi-billion-dollar organization. Or perhaps you are just starting your career, searching for opportunity. Whoever you are, wherever you are coming from, I believe you will see how my thoughts and inspirations, successes and failures, philosophies and real experiences can and will have an impact on you and your development as a Sales Assassin Master.

The challenge:

- ❖ Dig deep within yourself to become the best you can be!
- ❖ Discover your formula, passion, dedication and courage in each sales engagement!
- ❖ Become the Ultimate Sales Assassin!
- ❖ Welcome to the World of Sales Assassin Excellence!

CHAPTER 1

UNDERSTANDING CORPORATIONS AND SALES ORGANIZATIONS

COMPANIES ARE CONTINUOUSLY working with their sales organizations to address the most pressing challenges that exist in the marketplace:

- ❖ Improving Organizational Alignment and the Sales Process
- ❖ Identifying Critical Sales Indicators of Success
- ❖ Enhancing Sales Skills and Strategic Behaviors that Support Sales Success
- ❖ Building a Sales Coaching Culture
- ❖ Building and Embedding Sales Tools and a Support System that Drives Sustained Sales Performance

The sales function is like the unharnessed and unexplored world of space. There is so much we don't know and are learning each day. Sales organizations thrive in the chaos of what is the latest and greatest tool, technique or sales system. The chaos is real, the competition is fierce and bodies of those who do not succeed in the business litter the hallways of every organization.

***

Wisdom from Anthony Caliendo, the Ultimate Sales Assassin

Your ability to maneuver within the chaos of a massive corporation requires the strength and willingness to at times fail before succeeding, but it also requires the corporation be willing to allow you to learn from your failures and for the corporation to realize that your failure is also the organization's failure.

Achieving great sales organizations and growing great sales professionals starts at the top of any organization. The best sales organization achieves success starting with the CEO and working down to achieve buy-in and a commitment from all elements of the organization. When the proper buy-in is achieved, risk and the challenges are minimized. It is at this point that sales organizations begin to transform themselves.

The Search for the Sales Assassins

The search for the best sales professionals is a search for those who have the mentality, mindset and commitment to become a Sales Assassin. You must remember that the best producers of sales performance are those who have the *SAM DNA—**Distinctive Nature to Achieve***. The SAM DNA belongs to those who will produce with or without the tools, training and resources of the biggest organizations. They have the instincts and out-perform the average person. Finding the best is not luck, it is about a search for the personality characteristics that differentiate success from failure. No matter the nature of your business or its size or characteristics, finding the sales professionals that possess qualities that ignite passion to succeed is an imperative. Sales professionals are a special breed no matter the industry. Are people to be sales people? Certainly there is the old saying that says this is the case, but I'm not convinced. What I do know and I will say over and over is that I've never seen a person grow up or go to college with a desire to be a sales professional. Further, are there any tools that accurately predict sales capability? I have been through a ton of personality profile tools in search of the one that best predicts success. I'm sorry—**there is no such tool that has the one and only formula to predict success.**

People Transformation Drives Success

When organizations struggle, transformation within the sales force is necessary. Change is never easy in an organization. When the economy is tight, sales professionals are the first to feel the pinch. The path to success is to consider how to transform the people business. The key to success will be the anticipation and a deep enrichment of the techniques that will change the dynamics around the business. In advance of the latest and greatest of new products and prior to any new pricing models and cost control initiative, the ability to anticipate the needs around sales people and transforming the sales force to a SAM mentality becomes the smartest change mechanism that you can discover.

I have proven that the need to change the impact of your sales process leads to changing how the sales function acts each and every day. This change is focused around the 9 belts of SAM success that we will discuss in the next chapters. This is a new framework that is focused on reducing the risks of failure that are seen each day in the sales industry.

Organizations and the sales professional have to be willing to embrace this new methodology. The most successful sales force is that in which the corporation has integrated the sales dynamic into the mainstream of all elements of the organization.

They realize that the SAM methodology demands a vigorous integration of sales professionals in the normal organization platform. The SAM methodology is not designed as a win/loss proposition but as a system that integrates SAM mastery in the operations process and the operations process with the sales dynamic. This is a very difficult shift in thinking.

The most successful business operations focus on three change ideas:

1. The sales function must be integrated with the rest of business. Sales cannot be an island of people working independent from all the other aspects of a corporation.

2. The sales function data, reports, ideas and concepts must be available and well understood by the organization and key stakeholders to determine how it impacts organizational decisions and the changes required for sales success.

3. The sales function cannot be successful when it is a source of confusion and chaos. It must be a stable function with stable professionals who are well prepared and fully appreciative of their work and how this work contributes to profitability.

The best organizations understand that the sales function does not succeed when it displays a theoretical approach to business. It must be integrated and understood as the lifeblood and revenue stream of the organization. When the marketplace changes, the sales function must demand changes to keep pace. The mechanism, processes and training of sales professionals cannot be static, but instead the tools and development of the workforce must at times go through painful transitions and efforts to modernize thinking. This modernization must be a tenacious effort of expansion of its business intelligence. Business intelligence is then cascaded down to sales professionals. It is this business intelligence that will create the platform for front-line Sales Assassin development.

The sales function is now prepared to lead organizational success with a relentless, outrageous approach to attacking the market place and providing the most differentiated approach to clients possible. The Sales Assassin Methodology will move your organization from the "hoopla chaos" of the past to a rhythmic precision for the future.

My Sales Assassin methodology reinforces that the demand for products, services and revenue drives the success of business performance. A Sales Assassin team of professionals knows they will either lead or get out of the way of progress—and get out of the organization. When they lead, there is outrageous potential for success. The word *outrageous* must be seen as a mandate for an aggressive approach. The organization must learn that failure to meet goals is not about the loss of the individual big sales opportunity, but instead it's about loss and misuse of all the resources that it took to get us to this place and time—misuse of manufacturing and engineering efforts, misuse and cost of inventory left in the warehouse. The Sales Assassin is always seeking to better understand how the sales force WILL perform, rather than how it hopes and prays it will perform.

Finally, any successful organization must be focused on a stellar sales methodology that is customized to meet the organization's needs. The process must be integrated and aligned with all the other aspects of the business. Organizations may have within their sights a well crafted structure and significant investment in a sales method and sales leadership training, but then discover that the investment results in laborious work and a low ROI. The bottom-line is exact. Success for your organization demands a fully integrated approach to sales with the rest of the organization. The Sales Assassin approach is an intensive change mechanism, clearly focused on the people assets of your business.

Lessons From the Ultimate Sales Assassin Master:

1. The best producers of sales performance are those who have the *SAM DNA—**Distinctive Nature to Achieve***. The SAM DNA belongs to those who will produce with or without the tools, training and resources of the biggest organizations.

2. The sales function is like the unharnessed and unexplored world of space. There is so much we don't know and are learning each day.

3. Sales organizations thrive in the chaos of the latest and greatest tool, technique or sales system. The chaos is real, the competition is fierce and bodies of those who do not succeed in the business litter the hallways of every organization.

CHAPTER 2

SAM BELT 1:
PASSION, DEDICATION, COURAGE

"Passion is one of the most powerful engines of success. When you do a thing, do it with all your might. Put your whole soul into it. Stamp it with your own personality. Be active, be energetic and faithful, and you will accomplish your objective. Nothing great was ever achieved without passion."[6]
—Ralph Waldo Emerson

***

IN THE MARTIAL arts, the great masters of the art were in constant search for the students who demonstrated the characteristics of which Emerson speaks. The masters who selected students for Shaolin Temple demanded a great commitment from students. They were tested in the face of horrendous conditions. Some were eliminated while others continued the journey to Master Level acceptance. This commitment to passion, dedication and courage was told in stories from the great Zen Master Bodhidharma.

***

---

6   Maiers, Angela, 2012. The 5 C's of Passion Driven Leadership, http://www.angelamaiers.com/2012/01/the-5-cs-of-passion-driven-leadership.html

Zen Master Bodhidharma's successor, Hui-K'o, was born in 487 AD and journeyed to the Shaolin Temple at age 40 in order to meet the great Zen Master Bodhidharma.

Hui-K'o saw Bodhidharma meditating quietly and so waited until the master noticed him. As he waited it began snowing, but he simply stood there, until the snow reached his knees. Bodhidharma then asked him what he wanted, and Hui-K'o said "nothing, except to become your pupil."

Bodhidharma answered, "What I have been practicing asks for painstaking efforts. It is impossible for one who does not have the will and the courage; to him it will only be wasted effort and much suffering."

At this Hui-K'o pulled out his sword and cut off his left arm and presented it to Bodhidharma as proof of his serious intent. Moved by this Bodhidharma accepted him as a pupil. Upon Bodhidharma's death, Hui-K'o received his robe and alms bowl, so making him the second patriarch of Chan (Zen) in China.[7]

—Harry Cook, British, martial artist, teacher, and author

***

The art of mastering SAM status does not require you to cut off your arm to demonstrate your commitment, but it does require **Outrageous Passion, Dedication and Courage (PDC)** to persevere the greatest of obstacles. Your Distinctive Nature to Achieve is grounded in PDC. PDC is the holy trinity of the sales professional's heart, mind and spirit. It will drive success in the best and worst of times. Although PDC is an internal mindset, it is visible to everyone around you in the swagger of your walk and the way you talk. We have all heard that the 3 keys to success in the

---

7   Ford, James Etsujo. *Boundless Way of Zen*, http://www.boundlesswayzen.org/teishos/secretteachings. html

restaurant business are "location, location, location." Likewise, 3 keys to becoming successful in sales and further, to become a SAM is Passion, Dedication and Courage. These are core to forming your SAM DNA—Your *"Distinctive Nature to Achieve."*

PDC is a set of strong emotions and confidence that will move you past your comfort area—the area that most often brings the salesman to a screeching halt. These emotions and confidence come from reinvesting in yourself and especially your attitude, finding exceptional ways to do your work. This winning attitude has to come from your heart and mind and your spirit. This SAM element is the pure emotion that helps you realize and drive through and beyond your potential. I cannot teach you Passion, Dedication and Courage, but I can assist you in finding yours.

***

Wisdom from Anthony Caliendo, the Ultimate Sales Assassin

Passion, Dedication and Courage should be the energy that fuels you each day. This energy can be the powerful excitement that drives your ambitions. Success is the realization of your ambitions.

Developing the Passion

During my entire life I have soul-searched in an effort to unleash my passion—to tap into the type of passion necessary to soar to new heights and to the highest levels possible.

Passion is a word we love to say we have, but do we really have it, know it and feel it?

- Where does it come from?

- Where is it going and where can it take us?

- Are we born with it?

- Do we learn it?

- Do we build up to it?

- Or does it just happen in special moments of our lives?

For the sales professional, where does passion come from? We find our passions by finding meaning in life. **What is your meaning in life, what matters to you, what do you aspire to?** Throughout your life, what were the moments when you experienced the most passion, the most meaning and the most desire? And why? Another way to understand this point is to ask yourself what are the passions in your world that will *keep* you passionate. What are the passions in my world? The answer for me is simple. My passion is ME; me and every person or project or every endeavor that flows through me and around me. It is having a wholehearted conviction that whatever I decide to pursue I'm going to be the best at it. I exercise my passion every day by focusing on my vision. The underlying theme of everything I do is all about starting with an idea, adding some hope and ingenuity, and zeroing in on my vision of passionately building it, watching it come to fruition and being the very best at it. Effectually, I live with this conviction and passion because I am passionate about every aspect of my family and my children. However, when I think about myself as an individual I know that my true inner passion is all about making a mark, making an impression and making a difference not only for my family but for my businesses, the people who help me run my businesses and for my community.

Passion is to motivation as motivation is to passion. In other words, your passion develops once you determine what matters to you and where your motivation lies. For instance, if making a lot of money is your passion, then you will use that as your motivation. If your product or your service or your belief in what you do is your passion, then it becomes the basis for your motivation.

There is that rare individual whose passion is innate and they don't have to find it. These are the professionals with the right DNA—Distinctive Nature to Achieve. This individual has passion in everything they do, in their personal life and in their business realm. Kudos to this person, for he or she has probably already found success and found the way to sustain it.

Exercise

Identify 2 moments when your passion for something drove you to success. List one personal moment and one professional moment and state why and what drove you to success:

1. _____

2. _____

Passion Selling

Great sales people must have great passion, not sometimes, but all of the time, every day, hour, second! Why do some sales people live each day for potential success? What creates the distinction between that person achieving great things and that person who is constantly struggling to achieve? It's that the successful people have seized their sales opportunities (no matter what they are) and have learned to channel that inner passion and excitement about what they are doing. Simply put, great sales people must have great passion not sometimes but all of the time, every day and every hour of the day! Once you understand how absolutely important the role passion plays in selling, then the sky's the limit!

Television has become saturated with reality shows. There are Idols and X-Factors, Housewives and Mob Wives. We keep up with celebrities and have become guiltless voyeurs of countless wars: storage wars, survival wars, cooking wars, fashion wars, and love wars—the list goes on and on. I normally totally tune out to this stuff, but I do occasionally tune in when a certain real estate sales show comes on featuring these 3 guys who sell million dollar plus apartments in New York City. Talk about passion: these guys are off the charts. I realized that their entire success is about passion, dedication and courage. Their passion for what they do is indescribable. What I realized is that they are not necessarily smarter than other real estate agents, but their success is based on their drive, love and passion for what they do. Most intriguing is Fredrik, an obnoxious 35ish guy who sees the world and every opportunity as his and only his. Selfish yes, self-centered yes and passionate about his job, his products, and passionate and confident that there is no one better than him. Fredrik's success begins by demonstrating his passion to each potential client, his passion for their apartment and for meeting their specific needs and expectations. He then conveys and transfers his passion for his client and their property to perspective brokers and buyers. There is nothing that stands in this guy's way and nothing that destroys his passion for success. Fredrik is a Sales Assassin Master—a heat-seeking missile filled with PDC.

Passion is necessary in our attitudes. Equally, passion is one of the most important keys when it comes to relaying your product or service to your prospect. If you have a passionate attitude about your job then you will adopt that same passion for your product or service. You must feel a relationship with your product, no matter what it is. It means getting to know your product, becoming intimate with it and having a relentless belief in its benefits so that when you speak about it, that passion and energy projects from your gut, out of your mouth and into the minds of your customer!

When a salesperson is passion selling, selling is so fluid that it's not even selling anymore. Selling is no longer an effort, it has become second nature, and it has become natural and comfortable. In order to become a SAM you must learn and apply the concept of passion selling where the passion sweats from every pore of your body.

I had a conversation with my oldest son, Steven when he purchased his Apple computer. He was so ecstatic about his purchase, had become so well versed in its features, was so absolutely convinced about why it trumped other computers that when he spoke to me about it I wanted to run out and buy one for myself (and I didn't even need a new computer)! His demeanor and intonation was so darn fascinating to watch. He was selling that Apple computer without ever realizing it because he was so passionate about it. THAT'S PASSION SELLING and he's not a sales guy! If I had my eyes closed I might have thought I was talking to Fredrik the real estate guy. He should have saved his money when he got his Master Mechanic certification and went to Apple to be their top products sales person that very minute!

This is the strength of passion in sales! If the passion is strong, then you don't have to try. Your presentation is so believable because it is conveyed in such a way whereby you don't have to sell. Think about it this way. As a salesperson, when you "sell," your prospect senses that and you're actually perceived as the "pushy salesperson." Guess what, the new generation of customers does not want to be sold. I respect used car salespeople tremendously, but that old stigma surrounding that industry is one that most customers try to avoid. I'm here to inform you that nobody buys from someone they don't like. When your prospect signs on the dotted line, it's because he or she believes that you're sold on your own product's benefits and its ability to benefit them as well (and because you were likable).

Without question, you cannot and will not achieve this maximum level of sales ability without passion! Sales passion and passion in general is something you either have or don't have and it can come and go like the sun and the moon. It's up to you to figure out how to create it and how to keep it alive. For starters, you must focus on your goals, find out where your motivation lies and keep it real with yourself! If your passion truly is your product and you believe it is the best most beneficial product or service for businesses and/or consumers, then your prospects will undoubtedly hear that passion, confidence and sincerity in your presentation. If you know that success is your passion, no matter what sales opportunity you have been given, no matter if you're entry level looking to aspire to that "corner glass office" or if you're a "veteran sales person," then your desire for success will be the constant which drives you every single day.

Passion: From the Real Italian Stallion

Rocky Marciano, the original and real "Italian Stallion" is the only World Heavyweight Champion in boxing history to go undefeated or untied during his entire career. At a simple 5'11" and 185 lbs., Marciano was able to defeat his opponents by delivering his infamous "Suzy Q" right hand to overcome his size and reach disadvantage. Marciano is consistently ranked as one of the top ten heavyweight champions of all time. Even with staggering stats, it has been argued that Marciano was only able to hold on to the title because he never faced quality opponents. However, the point is that Marciano didn't recuse himself from the sport simply because of the sport's lack of talented fighters at the time. He continued to defend his title with the same passion and veracity as ever because he was a true champion, a true warrior at heart—a true winner.

***

Finding your sales Passion, Dedication and Courage is not always easy, but you need to understand how it works. In combination with one another the PDC trinity not only lights our fire but it has continuous hot coals burning beneath us and within us. It also gives power and energy to others and it will give power and energy even to your customers. I always ask my audiences to close their eyes for a moment and think about their greatest, most inspiring teacher, coach or boss. Then I ask them to write three words that best describes them. I am always amazed when I poll the room and ask how many people wrote some form of the word "passion" and the word "dedication". Passion, Dedication and Courage makes an impression on us and we feel it and see it in others. But what we feel and see in people with passion, dedication and courage comes from their heart and it penetrates the heart and spirit of others around them. This is the beginning step of creating a value proposition for customers and for the corporation. It is through PDC that you will make a lasting impact and begin to create exceptional results.

Passion, Dedication and Courage are enduring characteristics of the great samurai, athletes, our soldiers and those that are superior achievers who understand the concept of winning. PDC is an aspect of SAM that you ignite: the embers stay in you and in tough times can be reignited on a moment's notice. The SAM is not distracted when your Passion, Dedication and Courage are in gear. When I find that gear, lookout: I'm in "the zone" and nothing is going to stop me.

Exercise
Developing the Dedication

Are you really dedicated to what you do? Do you have a "self-sacrificing" devotion to your work or are you just pacifying yourself with your current job hoping something better will come along? STOP reading for 30 seconds and complete this exercise. What are 3 things that you have a "self-sacrificing" devotion to support or to achieve?

1. _____

2. _____

3. _____

If it took you longer than 30 seconds to answer this question, you should question if you are truly dedicated to these things. Most people immediately say their number one dedication is to family. That answer comes in seconds. Why? The reason is that we have clarity around family and realize our dedication. And in this case it is linked also to a passion and love for family. Was your job one of your 3 answers? Why? How long did it take for you to list your job? Why did you list your job as something you are dedicated to?

We can be dedicated to our jobs for many reasons:

- Because it is a source of security for you and your family

- Because you have a passion for the mission the job represents

- Because you have been dedicated to building a skill that you enjoy and the job provides you an opportunity to use the skill

Regardless of your rationale, dedication is another one of the more important must haves when it comes to getting ahead in your career and to getting ahead in life. You must be dedicated to a cause and to what you do on a daily basis. Without dedication, your outcomes are pretty predictable—predictably bleak. Realize that dedication and passion are two different things. They do not automatically link together. I believe that a majority of people do not have a problem or difficulty in being dedicated to their job but the challenge is how they will convert the dedication to passion.

You might ask yourself, how can I dedicate myself to anything worthwhile (i.e. my career, my life) when I'm constantly faced with challenges, setbacks, and obstacles? To the contrary, it's *dedication* that allows you to forge ahead and overcome daily challenges! Staying dedicated must be a mission like a straight and narrow path that you must constantly walk; having unbreakable faith that true dedication will lead you to becoming the best and having success, no matter what challenges or setbacks you face.

True dedication is total immersion. You have to go "all in" like Texas Hold 'Em! And as much as you'd like to justify being non-committed by making excuses about not having fair opportunities in life and the like, until you can commit to being "all the way in" you'll never achieve the success leading you to your "Promised Land."

Your lifeline in sales absolutely depends on being able to be 100% dedicated to the job. In order to become a SAM, you must find a way to accept adversities and setbacks as a part of the sales process and then manifest that level of dedication that helps you move forward with your objectives. Realize: there are certain action items you must focus on in order to stay dedicated and they revolve around "personal professional" enrichment. Are you taking the time to learn, for example, how to be a better salesperson, how to have a better attitude, how to take responsibility for your rises as well as your falls, how to have more passion? If not, ask yourself why and figure out what you need to do to change your thinking because figuring out what you're dedicated to be is absolutely integral and essential while you're walking down that straight and narrow path.

Dedication Challenge Exercise:

Define an occasion when you became dedicated and driven to accomplish a goal over an extended period of time. Define what you were so dedicated to. Was it money or was it an internal desire for success?

1. What was the focus of your dedication? What did you want to achieve?

   _____

   _____

2. What was your motivation to achieve this goal? Money, pride etc.

   _____

   _____

3. Were there things that distracted you and lessened your commitment?

   _____

   _____

What differentiates a SAM from the conventional sales person is his or her dedication to the job and passion they have to drive through the most difficult times. It truly sets him or her apart from their counterparts. Don't cheat yourself or your company by maintaining a lackadaisical, undedicated approach to your craft. Your sales performance will definitely show it! Not every sales person is fortunate enough to work in an environment where he or she can thrive, where management willingly and graciously gives its sales staff every sales tool accessible, or where personal goals are fostered and nurtured. If you want success, you must seize every opportunity to demonstrate your hard work and dedication. Not only is it infectious, but your superiors will notice, your customers will notice, and the people in your life will notice. Effectually, success is in the palm of your hand both professionally and personally.

***

"We've all heard about people who've exploded beyond the limitations of their conditions to become examples of the unlimited power of the human spirit.
You and I can make our lives one of these legendary inspirations, as well, simply by having courage and the awareness that we can control whatever happens in our lives. Although we cannot always control the events in our lives, we can always control our response to them, and the actions we take as a result.
If there's anything you're not happy about—in your relationships, in your health, in your career—make a decision right now about how you're going to change it immediately."[8]
—Tony Robbins

A Lesson in Life: Overcoming Defeat

I remember when I was transitioning out of the health club business and into the stockbroker profession, I was faced with one of my greatest professional challenges. Anyone desiring to be a stockbroker in the U.S. must take the General Securities Representative Examination, which is often referred to as the Series 7 or Stockbroker Exam. The exam is a six-hour test of your knowledge, skills and integrity. I didn't realize how difficult and how much dedication I had to put into this exam, in order to pass.

During this time, I was going to school and studying for the test,

---

8   Goodreads. https://www.goodreads.com/author/quotes/5627.Anthony_Robbins

leaving one business and trying to get my license for a new business. I studied relentlessly and remember there was so much material to learn in a short period of time. I was never a person who found it easy to study and retain information in preparation for a test. But I am smart, I study and I'm always committed. This test was going to take all my strength and dedication. I spent months studying to prepare for a business I knew nothing about.

The first time I took the test, I failed by 3 points. I was disappointed and upset because I know how much time and effort I put into trying to pass. I went back to the drawing board and started again and studied harder—more time, more effort , 3 more months of agony. My bank account was draining. I was stressed and overwhelmed, but it was time to take the test again. I failed again—one point from passing. I was more than upset. Everything and all of the hard work meant nothing because I could not pass the test. I had never had that feeling, because I had never accepted or had to deal with defeat.

Nevertheless, I would not be defeated. By the time my third attempt at this test came around, I was losing everything. I owned my own house, cars, and motorcycle and now I was watching all my hard work being swept away. My lights were getting shut off, my cars were in jeopardy of getting repossessed. I was at the bottom. But I studied even harder this time. I went to the library and studied 12 hours a day. I was there from open to close.

The day came for the 3ʳᵈ test. If I didn't pass, the rules say that I would have had to wait another 6 months before I could re-test. I just couldn't afford defeat. I passed with a 70 and got my Series 7 license. This was probably the most dedicated I have been in my life when it came to not allowing myself to stop. I pushed when most would quit and say "it's not for me" and give up. Dedication is what separates success from failure.

In sales, you must learn to be 100% dedicated to what you're doing. You have to be dedicated in a way that sets you apart from everybody else. Your hard work and dedication will propel you to a level you cannot imagine. Most people go through life, giving up when things don't work out and they simply give up. Dedication is what sets you apart from everybody else.

We all know negative people. They come into work negative, constantly unhappy, acting like everything around them is everyone else's fault and that's why they cannot succeed. They are no longer dedicated. You have to have a straight path that you constantly pursue, that you truly believe that if you dedicate enough time and effort ,you will become the best.

Many salespeople do not have sufficient dedication. They don't immerse themselves. They don't go all the way in. Like Texas Hold 'Em, if you want to win, you have to be all in—all or nothing. Not once in a while, but all the time. This is what true dedication is all about. We constantly have obstacles thrown at us every day. Overcome them and move forward. Focus on your dedication to your job and your career! You're a salesperson! Truly you are selling yourself! Dedication is very important. Focus on it.

> *"Tough Times Never Last, But Tough People Do."*[9]
> —Dr. Robert Schuller

***

---

9   Philosiblog, 2011. http://philosiblog.com/2011/11/23/tough-times-never-last-but-tough-people-do/

Determining Your Courage

When courage is combined with passion and dedication the Sales Assassin becomes the victor of the sales wars, finding the means to persevere the odds, always able to leverage the forces around him or her—pros and cons. Courage is an immeasurable trait that is an instinctive ability to know when to gamble and the ability to feel comfortable with the odds of that gamble.

Courage is one of the most valuable traits you can have and develop as a salesperson and as a business professional. Courage is the ability to act in spite of fear. It's being able to do things when the fear would freeze a weaker man. And courage is a trait that can be developed. Developing courage is like building a muscle. You've got to exercise it, work it out, stretch it and stress it. And as long as you don't overdo it, your muscle will get stronger. This means taking risks, big enough ones to stretch yourself, but reasonable enough ones that you can succeed at them. Smarts and talent are overrated. There are plenty of smart, talented failures in the world, they keep hoping for success, and not understanding PDC is the answer. The SAM knows how to apply the ***20 Seconds of Insane Courage*** rule to every challenging sales engagement.

One of my favorite movies is *We Bought a Zoo*. In the movie, Benjamin Mee, played by Matt Damon, wants to instill courage and bravery in his children after the tragic loss of their mother. In one of the great scenes of the movie he says to his son, *"You know, sometimes all you need is twenty seconds of insane courage. Just literally twenty seconds of just embarrassing bravery. And I promise you, something great will come of it."*[10]

---

10   IMDb, 2011. We Bought a Zoo. http://www.imdb.com/title/tt1389137/quotes

Benjamin is right, however I believe a Sales Assassin finds 20 seconds of insane courage every hour of every day and they live a creed to search for Passion, Dedication and Courage as a way of life. However, even in the 20-second rule things go wrong, but PDC provides you the faith to remain strong and engage, knowing that you must do everything in your power to succeed, rather than relying on hope that things will work out. Passion, Dedication and Courage when properly applied will bring you whatever you want in this life and will allow you to succeed as a sales professional or within any other professional endeavor that you may choose.

The Trinity of Emotion

***

Finding Your PDC

PDC is not a trait that we can anticipate or predict because it will be self-discovered in each of us in a number of different ways. The first belt of Sales Assassin Mastery is not intended to be a formula that is predictable. It is a concept that kicks into gear, like a running back that moves with instinct, never knowing where danger or the next challenge will lurk. It permits an urgent response to challenges we face and gives us strength to endure.

There are six concepts that will help you understand and find your PDC:

1. **Plan:** Organize yourself and lay out a mental and physical plan for action.

2. **The Search and the Hunt:** Search for the opportunities. Find some small, quick wins for confidence.

3. **Engagement and Self Sacrifice:** You must find and feel a desire to act each day. You must find the resources in the form of people and process and connect with them and through them.

4. **Discipline:** The ability not to be discouraged when your plan is not going as designed. The ability to regroup and refocus your efforts.

5. **Risk Taking:** The ability to step beyond when others are guarded, cautious, and unwilling to go beyond the norm. You love the thrill of taking a chance and the adventure of the hunt.

6. **Continuous Improvement and Opportunity:** The ability to never be satisfied, continuously improve and continuously search for new opportunities and challenges.

PDC allows the difficult days and most challenging of circumstances to become energy for us. The challenges will become your fuel and fear will no longer constrain your ability to grow and succeed. Organizations teach sales skills each day, but can they teach courage? No, but I can help you realize it and discover what courage is to the sales process. The process of learning new things isn't hard, once you get started. And if you are afraid to get started, then of course you never learn. And you stay stuck "doing" the business, making products for it, prettying it up, but never getting enough customers.

Remember, the Sales Assassin Master will never be denied, for you will have achieved Passion, Dedication and Courage—your sword will be sharp and precise. You will move with precision and confidence through your sales journey. PDC is not a balancing act. PDC will always outweigh fear!

Passion, Dedication and Courage In The Words of Great Leaders:

- **Sun Tzu, author of *The Art of War*,** an ancient Chinese military treatise, quoted in many leadership and business books, underscored the importance of passion, *"Soldiers who care about their cause fight harder. Their passion invites support. They turn the world on their side."*[11]

- **Nelson Mandela,** the South African anti-apartheid revolutionary, politician, and philanthropist who served as President of South Africa from 1994 to 1999 said, "I learned that courage was not the absence of fear, but the triumph over it. The brave man is not he who does not feel afraid, but he who conquers that fear."[12]

---

11   Unlimited Success Blog, 2012. What is your passion? Who do you want to be? What do you want to do with your life?, http://www.unlimited-success.co.uk/blog/what-is-your-passion/

12   Nsehe, Mfonobong, 2013. 19 *Inspirational Quotes From Nelson Mandela,* http://www.forbes.com/sites/mfonobongnsehe/2013/12/06/20-inspirational-quotes-from-nelson-mandela/

- **Steve Jobs,** the great visionary of the Apple empire said, "Your time is limited, so don't waste it living someone else's life. Don't be trapped by dogma—which is living with the results of other people's thinking. Don't let the noise of others' opinions drown out your own inner voice. And most important, have the courage to follow your heart and intuition."[13]

- **Mihaly Csikszentmihalyi,** the psychologist said, *"Passion is the feeling of total engagement in the activity so that you don't notice anything outside of what you're doing."*[14]

- **Richard Branson,** founder of Virgin Group, says of passion, *"If you're into kite-surfing and you want to become an entrepreneur, do it with kite-surfing. Look, if you can indulge in your passion, life will be far more interesting than if you're just working. You'll work harder at it, and you'll know more about it. But first, you must go out and educate yourself on whatever it is that you've decided to do—know more about kite-surfing than anyone else. That's where the work comes in. But if you're doing things you're passionate about, that will come naturally."*[15]

13   Vaillancourt, Marc, 2011. *Steve Jobs: Your Time is Limited, Don't Waste It,* http://theconversationhub. com/steve-jobs-your-time-is-limited-dont-waste-it/

14   Russell, Leigh, 2012. *It's Easier With Passion,* http://www.leighrussell.com.au/tag/passion/

15   Krippendorff, Kaihan, 2012. *How to Find Your Passion Workbook,* www.Kaihan.com

Finding Your PDC Balance

The Ultimate Fighter—Passion Dedication Courage

About 15-20 years ago, I started getting into the new age sport and style of fighting, known as Mixed Martial Arts (MMA) and the promotion company that catapulted it into the mainstream, The Ultimate Fighting Championship (UFC). Naturally, I was drawn because of my own martial arts training, but mostly because I enjoy the physical and psychological rivalry of combat sports. The history of the UFC tells a very interesting story.

The very first UFC competition served one, distinct purpose; to determine once and for all which fighting discipline is the most effective in a real combat situation. A by-product of that determination was if skill, technique and tactics could defeat pure size and brute strength.

At UFC 1, ultimate warriors representing every fighting style from boxing, kickboxing and wrestling to Brazilian Jiu-Jitsu, Karate and Judo were recruited to compete in the event. UFC co-founder, Rorion Gracie hand selected his brother Royce Gracie, a Brazilian Jiu-Jitsu black belt to fight in the competition, not only to showcase his immense skill level and family legacy in the art, but also because he was a meager 175 lbs. to his 250-400 lb. opponents. Pay-per-view fight fans watched in anticipation as these warriors stepped into The Octagon™ in a no-holds-barred, unregulated, and what some would call barbaric submission matches.

What happened was revolutionary. Royce Gracie dominated UFC 1, proving that size and strength does not necessarily prevail over skill and technique. Gracie maintained domination between UFC 1 and UFC 4 and from that a hypothetical became law. Fighters started cross training in different disciplines and became skilled in different types of fighting styles. Modern day MMA was born and the UFC emerged from an unregulated, banned in thirty-six states sport into a sanctioned, legitimized, mainstream phenomenon.

Not everyone reading this book will be a fan of the UFC. But, as an Ultimate SAM, I believe its history; its organization, its ultimate warriors and the entire UFC culture demonstrates an outrageous example of tenacity, strength and PDC.

Dana White, current UFC President along with Zuffa, LLC owners Lorenzo and Frank Fertitta, took the sport from obscenity and virtual obscurity to a global brand, broadcasted today in 19 languages to more than 1 billion homes in 148 countries.[16] UFC color commentator Joe Rogan (former host of Fear Factor), also a 2nd Degree Black Belt in Taekwondo and a Black Belt in Brazilian Jiu-Jitsu is a master at commentary because of his lifelong passion and dedication to martial arts. These fighters have to be trained and skilled in multiple disciplines and must make the transformation from "man to machine" before they're considered fit for The Octagon.™ The UFC demands of these modern day gladiators unrelenting Passion, Dedication and Courage and their name in blood that they will remain mentally and emotionally voracious.[17]

Lessons From the Ultimate Sales Assassin Master:

1. Nothing can be created in your life without your passion for the product and your passion for who you are and what you want to be.

2. Dedication is first focused on your willingness to self-sacrifice and to commit to allowing your passion to flourish and be realized.

3. With courage we have an ability to be mentally or morally strong and be willing to venture, persevere, and able to withstand danger of failure and the fear of failure.

4. We need 20 seconds of insane courage every minute, of every hour, of every day.

---

16 (http://www.bloomberg.com/news/2012-08-01/fertittas-made-billionaires-by-head-blows-with-chokeholds.html).

17 (http://www.ufc.com/discover/fighter/what-it-takes.html).

A Sales Assassin Master Challenge

Self-Discover your abilities and control in **SAM Passion, Dedication and Courage: Belt 1**

1. How do you perform against each of the PDC competencies?

Scale: 5 = SAM, 4 = Evolving to a SAM, 3 = SAM is my Goal
2 = I'm Struggling, 1 = I'm failing as a sales professional

    a. _____**Plan:** Organize yourself and lay out a mental and physical plan for action.

    b. _____**The Search and the Hunt:** Search for the opportunities.

    c. _____**Engage:** You must find and feel a desire to act each day. You must find the resources in the form of people and process and connect with them and through them.

    d. _____**Discipline:** The ability not to be discouraged when your plan is not going as designed. The ability to regroup and refocus your efforts.

    e. _____**Risk Taking:** The ability to step beyond when others are guarded and cautious and unwilling to go beyond the norm. You love the thrill of taking a chance and the adventure of the hunt.

    f. _____**Continuous Improvement and Opportunity.**

2. How do others view your performance against each of the PDC competencies?

Scale: 5 = SAM, 4 = Evolving to a SAM, 3 = SAM is my Goal
2 = I'm Struggling, 1 = I'm failing as a sales professional

    a. _____**Plan:** Organize yourself and lay out a mental and physical plan for action.

b. _____**The Search and the Hunt:** Search for the opportunities.

c. _____**Engage:** You must find and feel a desire to act each day. You must find the resources in the form of people and process and connect with them and through them.

d. _____**Discipline:** The ability not to be discouraged when your plan is not going as designed. The ability to regroup and refocus your efforts.

e. _____**Risk Taking:** The ability to step beyond when others are guarded and cautious and unwilling to go beyond the norm. You love the thrill of taking a chance and the adventure of the hunt.

f. _____**Continuous Improvement and Opportunity:** The ability to grow and learn from success and failure.

3. In your SAM journey, I'm sure you are proud of certain things and not so proud of others. Be specific: Who, What, When, Where, Why?

a. What are you proud of?

_____

b. What would you like to have done differently?

_____

c. How do your customers respond to you?

_____

4. What is the gap between your PDC levels today and your PDC vision for the future? Which of these steps defines your

greatest opportunity for improvement and why?

a. _____**Plan:** Organize yourself and lay out a mental and physical plan for action.

b. _____**The Search and the Hunt:** Search for the opportunities.

c. _____**Engage:** You must find and feel a desire to act each day. You must find the resources in the form of people and process and connect with them and through them.

d. _____**Discipline:** The ability not to be discouraged when your plan is not going as designed. The ability to regroup and refocus your efforts.

e. _____**Risk Taking:** The ability to step beyond when others are guarded and cautious and unwilling to go beyond the norm. You love the thrill of taking a chance and the adventure of the hunt.

f. _____**Continuous Improvement and Opportunity:** The ability to grow and learn from success and failure.

_____

_____

_____

_____

Passion Dedication Courage Exercise

Know Your Strengths As a Sales Professional—*What are you good at?*

If you find yourself to be good at something, chances are you'll become at least a little fond of that subject. It works in two ways actually; we try harder to be good at things that we are fond of and we like the things that we are good at. It's sort of a ***positive vicious circle*** that's definitely worth getting into. Assessing your strengths makes it easier to narrow down the subjects that you would naturally be good at, and that way, also naturally ***like***. Answer these questions and be honest with yourself.

1. As a sales professional what are the skills that you feel you are really good at doing?

   _____

   _____

   _____

2. Are you passionate about doing these things? Yes or No

3. Do you put extra effort into the things you do very well? Yes or No

4. As a sales professional, what are the skills that you feel you do NOT do well?

   _____

   _____

   _____

5. Are you passionate about doing these things?   Yes or No

6. Do you put extra effort into the things?   Yes or No

Generally speaking, most people put far more effort into the things they naturally do well. I'll bet you answered question 5 as a big NO. We become more passionate about things we do well and can feel the potential for success. This is a natural result. However, the real challenge and the thing that really takes our sales performance to the next level is to be committed to the things we do NOT do well. This can be a tough venture, but if we can put time into improving our weaknesses, we will become more passionate about them. They will become new strengths and new passions within your sales life. This is a cornerstone lesson you will discover in the chapters to come.

CHAPTER 3

SAM BELT 2:
MENTAL PREPAREDNESS
DEVELOPMENT

"Being challenged in life is inevitable, being defeated is optional."[18]
—Roger Crawford

PRIOR TO THE start of the 2013 US Open Golf Tournament, Phil Mickleson was on an airplane traveling back to Philadelphia for his first round of the tournament. He had made a 24-hour round trip home to California for his daughter's graduation. Reporters were sure this would be a disadvantage—not spending precious time hitting balls on such a challenging course. Not to Phil, "I think that mental preparation is every bit as important as physical," he told reporters. "I was able to take the time on the plane to read my notes, study, relive the golf course, go through how I was going to play each hole, where the pins were, where I want to miss it, where I want to be, study the green charts." Mickelson didn't win the tournament, but he sure came close and his 7 AM first round performance demonstrated his point with an under par performance. His entire journey defines his mental preparation and is evidence of what we have called the SAM DNA.

---

18   Goodreads. http://www.goodreads.com/quotes/496796-being-challenged-in-life-is-inevitable-being-defeated-is-optional

We are all familiar with the idea of aerobic conditioning, exercise designed to train the heart and lungs to pump blood more efficiently. Likewise, the SAM definition of mental conditioning is the act of preparing and training the mind to receive, absorb and retain ideas and processes more efficiently. In order to become a SAM, you have to train and develop yourself and grasp the notion of mental conditioning as an integral part of your overall growth.

When I'm speaking at a sales meeting, convention or seminar, I'm always scanning the audience, reading their mood, evaluating their attitude, and assessing what's going through their minds. I can instantly identify those individuals who appear to be engaged and prepared to receive the message versus those individuals who have come with skeptical expectations about what they are going to hear and probably excuses for what they expect of themselves. I can even see the difference in their posture: their facial expressions are clear and evident. Sometimes it's as simple as the difference between the individual who is sitting erect, pad and pen in hand versus the one who's sitting back with his arms folded over his chest. This second group of individuals is guilty of having a defensive attitude, or for lack of a better phrase the "I just don't want to be here" syndrome.

Let's face it, in sales you are forever bound to the notion of the "never-ending sales meetings and seminars" phenomenon. Meetings and seminars are to sales like Sunday "gravy" is to being Italian-American. We are inundated with it; it is a fact of our lives. If it's not a meeting or a seminar, it's a book, a manual, a blog or even just a conversation with a co-worker or a manager where ideas and philosophies are shared. However, no matter what the platform or venue, you will never be able to gain useful knowledge without what I call mental preparedness or conditioning.

In any field of endeavor, the mind is a core component of success. It must be conditioned and prepared to engage every challenge in life. The mind is a strong instrument when it is developed and unleashed to its full capacity. When your mind is conditioned and prepared properly great things are possible. When your mind is not properly conditioned and ready, you are not prepared to handle the difficult situations and challenges that life presents. More importantly, your *mental preparedness is a core aspect of any sales endeavor*. The sales world is one of continuous stress and demand for performance. We can only manage this stress with mental preparation. Unfortunately, this is typically the last aspect of our life that we think of conditioning. Therefore, you must understand that when you have not taken the effort to mentally prepare, you will not overcome the natural adversity, failures, indecision and panic that you will eventually face as a human.

> *"Success is not to be measured by the position someone has reached*
> *in life-but the obstacles he has overcome while trying to succeed."*[19]
> —Booker T. Washington

***

What do I want you to be mentally prepared to do and what does it involve? Quite simply, I want you to be prepared to *"learn how to learn."* Learning how to learn literally means going back to the basics and clearing your mind and doing some de-programming in order to make room for new ideas and concepts. Initially, this involves training and conditioning the mind to release any blockages that are hindering your learning process. These blockages could be preconceived notions, a pessimistic outlook about the information

---

19   The Literature Page. Booker T. Washington: Up From Slavery: An Autobiography http://www. literaturepage.com/read/upfromslavery-32.html

you are about to hear, fear of redundancy or even boredom. Realize that in sales, more often than not, your mind could be your biggest adversary if you allow it! If you can admit this to yourself from the very beginning, then you're on the right path to new mental conditioning and development.

Even as you read this book, are you doing so with an open mind, prepared to read about new techniques and new ideas? The fact that you are even reading this book indicates to me that you're craving to gain a new perspective on how to become a better sales person. Likewise, gaining that fresh perspective requires an open mind, ready to absorb new knowledge so that it can be applied and put to practical use. Merely reading this book from cover to cover doesn't guarantee that when you're finished you will become a SAM. But having willingness and desire to learn with the mental capacity to absorb and retain information will most certainly guarantee that you're in prime position to become one.

Any sales environment can and will illicit fear and intimidation. But you have to allow your mind to play the role in creating your interpersonal resolve to be resilient and drive away the anxiety and stress of the function. Mental preparedness is what supports our feelings of hope and also our confidence to drive forward through two steps of failure verses one step of success. It is your mental preparedness that will enable you to see another day in a new light.

The Sales Assassin uses a five-step process to establish Mental Preparation:

1. **Mind Conditioning:** Your mind will strengthen and become more resilient when you condition your body through a regular routine of exercise. The more consistent,

dedicated and engaging your physical routine the more your mind is also readied and prepared for the stress that you may endure on the job. Mental preparedness is also setting rules and standards for yourself:

a. What are the work habits and rituals that get your mind into an aggressive flow each day?

b. What are your eating habits that get you into a flow and energize you throughout the day?

c. What are your exercise habits each day?

d. What are your sleep and relaxation habits each day?

Each of these elements has a direct relation to your mental conditioning

2. **Attitudinal Conditioning:** Have you ever been told by someone that "Your attitude sucks?" Your daily attitude is part of your mental conditioning and therefore it too must be prepared. The University of Notre Dame football program is well known for its slogan "Play Like A Champion Today." This means play with the attitude of championship. This translates that as a SAM you have to "Sell Like A Champion," be a winner, talk like a winner and walk like a winner. Folks, it's in our attitude, it's in the swagger of our walk and the way we talk.

A winner's attitude of success is the result of being able to see things positively and being able to withstand a difficult scenario. A SAM has to be like a football team. No coach will ever allow his team on the field without insuring that they truly believe that they can and will win the game. Playing well or performing well does not happen by chance. You have to want it and you have to feel it.

3. **Visual Conditioning**: They see themselves as winners. Remember as a kid seeing yourself hitting the game winning homerun? There is no athlete that does not go through the mental process of visualizing being the star of the game. We all have those moments when we see ourselves at the ultimate moment of success. Mental conditioning is the ability to allow your mind to visualize what success looks like and feels like. You must visualize yourself engaged in the selling process through each step of the way to your desired level of success. You have to be able to see the success and see how you will deal with the turbulent times that will slam you in the worst of storms. You must visualize yourself succeeding, overcoming the bad, and taking advantage of the good. When I see these moments in my mind, they are more than a dream, they are real. I can feel success and I want to duplicate that feeling as often as possible.

4. **Education, Homework, Repetition**: Mental Preparation requires educating yourself to knowledge, ideas and possibilities. It takes researching not only your product or service area but also continuous education on how to think and behave. Continuous education demands repetition, and repetition conditions our brains to constantly engage and be prepared

5. **Conditioning Through Mental Trust:** In any sales environment, you are going to realize two irrefutable facts:

   1. Selling is not easy.

   2. You are tougher than you think.

   In general, people are tougher than they think and we have an uncanny ability to be resilient and the ability to adapt when mentally prepared. However, we must trust our instincts that we can persevere in any situation. Perhaps this is no different than persons who discover that they have survived disaster situations and are surprised to find that they never considered what they would do; they immediately found themselves stepping up to challenges and doing what had to be done. When we are prepared mentally, we will likely find no time to doubt ourselves and our ability to succeed.

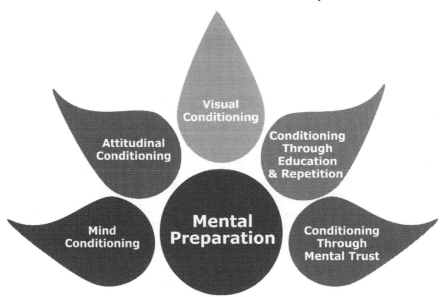

Being Mentally Prepared

The Sales Assassin Master realizes that you must:

- Not only maintain the will to survive, but the will to win, no matter what

- Use your brain as a tool of ingenuity to adapt to the situation

- Always look for opportunities to elevate yourself to higher levels of performance

- Refuse to concede to defeat or refuse to buy into beliefs such as I can't do it, I'm not smart enough to do it, I'm not good enough to do it, I'm powerless against this tough competition. The feeling of being powerless in any situation results in one of two options:

Option 1: Winning, success, drive and more ambition
Option 2: Defeat: I can't. It's not possible

In either situation, you do not know if your mind is right or wrong, good or bad. Your mind just responds how it has been conditioned and what it knows. It responds to your habits, attitudes and beliefs and these things have been conditioned. If as a SAM you imagine being strong and being decisive and controlling your fears and anxieties and acting rational, then your mind will only know to act this way in the future. However, if you imagine yourself hiding and afraid, then your mind acts in this manner. These fears can destroy your determination and confidence.

Example:

Professional Mixed Martial Arts fighters spend countless hours preparing for their next bout. They analyze their prior performances in their mind and study the video footage of theirs and their opponent's last matches, scrutinizing their opponent's strikes, counterstrikes and submission holds. They endure ruthless training drills to make their bodies tough, durable and impervious to pain and they sustain the most rigid diet and nutrition regimens in order to make or maintain weight. The night before the big fight they go through the plan of attack in their mind, preparing. They see the strikes, the movement, anticipating and envisioning their opponent's plan of attack, anticipating their own counter-attack and delivering crippling, ground and pound blows of defeat. Now it's "Fight Night" and he tries to execute his plan by shooting in on his opponent, but instead he is delivered a flying knee, collapses and his opponent finishes the fight with strikes, winning by TKO. The question is…what will the fighter do?

- Will he be dejected?
- Will he panic and question himself?
- Will he yell and scream at his trainers and coaches?

If he's a good fighter and mentally prepared, he will regroup when he gets back to the gym. He will talk to his trainers, his coaches and his camp to understand what went wrong. For example he or she will lay out a new plan of attack and then relax, take a deep breath and refocus his mind from what happened to what will happen the next time he steps into the cage. He is a SAM in this moment.

The Sales Assassin is focused on the things you CAN control with the proper mindset:

- Your daily schedule of work
- Understanding your products and services
- Developing and implementing your sales strategy
- The individualized approach to each client
- Visualizing the engagement, your words and actions, in response to different scenarios

Focusing on these types of preparations and the sales task in front of you will assist you in maintaining the right frame of mind. When a SAM finds himself struggling or losing a great client and begins to question the ability to succeed he or she should find new confidence by refocusing on his goals. Tom Hill, an expert in goal planning says,

> *"The key to any successful business plan is to first have a solid goal. From that goal you can develop a plan of action to reach the desired result. However, as soon as you set the plan in motion, life starts throwing you curve balls in the form of distractions, little challenges, and roadblocks in the path toward your goal. When you're surrounded by these distractions, your energy goes into "putting out the brush fires" and it's easy to lose your focus on the original goal. One fellow described it to me by saying, "when you're up to your tail in alligators, it's hard to remember that your original goal was to drain the swamp." This leads to what business consultants refer to as "crisis management" and soon the business is running you instead of you running the business."[20]*

One thing I know for sure is that we all face many alligator filled swamps. Your ability to manage your way through these swamps will not always be easy and it will take your ability to refocus on the things that matter and not sink and be swallowed by the dangers lurking.

---

20   Hill, Tom, 2000. Refocus on Your Business Plan and Regain Sight of Your Goals http://www.icsmag. com/articles/print/refocus-on-your-business-plan-and-regain-sight-of-your-goals

Refocus Plan Exercise:
Keeping Your Focus

Write out your goals in as much detail as you can. This helps you to visualize exactly where you want to go.

_____

_____

_____

Quantify all of your goals with measures that make sense to you in terms of weeks, months or a year—small chunks that you can see, touch and feel. Post these numbers where you will see them several times each day.

- If your goals are yearly, divide the number by either 12 (to get a monthly total), or 52 (to get a weekly goal) and post that number near the original number. This allows you to track your progress toward your goal.

_____

_____

_____

Write out the rewards that are at stake. Write out the reward you will earn from the company and those that you are going to give yourself—small rewards for weekly goals and larger rewards for meeting monthly and yearly goals.

_____

_____

_____

Identify and post pictures that represent those rewards where you will see them every day.

_____

_____

_____

Address challenges immediately when they arise and ask yourself if it meets one of the only two criteria that warrants your attention:

- Does the challenge hinder your opportunity for success?
- Can you control the obstacle or adjust to the obstacle to drive success?

_____

_____

_____

This technique focuses everything in terms of your business goals and keeps your focus on the goal. This is mental conditioning. It also allows you to put into perspective the true nature of the challenge or distraction. It may seem absolutely imperative that you deal with that alligator. However, if you think about it, there would be no alligators in a drained swamp, so drain the swamp that surrounds your mind. Keep your focus and meet your goals and the rest will fall into place.

The SAM goal is always to regroup and refocus forcing themselves to create a decisive plan on how to move forward. The Refocus Plan becomes the new goal with new determination that will focus on a new sales journey.

Is Sales Your Disaster Zone? Stop Being Defensive!

How often do you go into shock after a disastrous sales loss? I read an article about how people survive in disaster situations and realized how similar it is to how sales people feel when struggling for success. Of course, sales is not an immediate life or death struggle but it does create trauma and distress. I have watched sales professionals go into shock and not know how to deal with the challenge—succumbing to emotions. Fear consumes them just as fear consumes the disaster victim. The "Oh my god!" syndrome of disbelief, disorientation, and difficulty making decisions can be paralyzing. Tess Pennington wrote in her article **Are You Ready Series: Using Mental Preparedness to Survive** *"In a survival situation, a person feels these emotions for a reason, and those emotions are there to keep the person alive. Remember that using these feelings to a person's advantage is making good use of the situation as well as the energy that those emotion's are exerting."* The problem with sales people is it's too easy to yield to your emotions rather than using them to your advantage. It is your mental preparedness that will assist in controlling you and your next steps. Pennington adds,

> *"Stress, fear and anxiety are all associated as negative and destructive emotions. However, these could make a person more alert of the situation, stimulate and motivate a person to perform at their very best levels. The emotions will not only take advantage of a person's strengths, but will work on one's weaknesses and the ability to face their fears. A person must confront and manage these emotions head on in order to keep up their momentum and to not go into panic mode."[21]*

---

21 Pennington, Tess. Are You Ready Series: Using Mental Preparedness to Survive http://readynutrition. com/resources/are-you-ready-series-using-mental-preparedness-to-survive_26082013/

Figuratively and literally, get off the defense! Get rid of the defensive posture and get rid of the defensive attitude. To continue to be on the defensive means you are limiting your own growth and development. You're impeding your own progress and sabotaging your own success. You have to train yourself to stifle those voices inside your head that cause your defensive behaviors. Tell those inner voices to shut up and stop talking so that you can start listening to new ideas! Remember in Sales 101 when you learned that in order to be successful in sales you have to learn how to listen to your customer in order to qualify them properly? Well, I'm challenging you to qualify yourself! Who are you? What do you need and want to become? How will you get there? Guess what, you can't hear the answers if you're not listening to the messages and not paying attention to the opportunities presenting themselves to you!

Yes, it might take a lot of energy and a lot of discipline to be open minded and receptive all of the time. But the more you put this technique into practice, the more you condition your mind to these positive behaviors; you will reap the benefits, guaranteed! The next time you have to attend a meeting or a seminar with your new "mind in training," (because face it, there will be more sales meetings in your future), exercise your ability to sit back, listen intently and take in any information that might actually benefit you. Accepting the fact that you are going to hear some redundant concepts and information that you've already heard only allows you to fine tune your senses to pick up on that one little idea that you may have never heard before. Oprah refers to it as your "A-ha moment!" Mental preparedness will lead you to experience countless "A-ha moments" of the life-changing, attitude altering kind.

Becoming a SAM demands a mentally conditioned mind, prepared for peak sales performance in order to propel you to the next level! A Sales Assassin Master stays focused on how you can and must improve your situation. They search for mental and physical ways to take fear of failure out of possibilities, leaving room to begin to develop a Refocus Plan. Remember this is not a plan of escape but rather a plan of actions and solutions. There is always a way out. There are always a multitude of solutions that someone can find. Focusing on what is important in a person's life and clinging to that thought with all of their might will help lead them out of danger. *We all tend to lose hope at one time or another due to the uncertainties that lie ahead. Sitting down and writing the information out will also help you feel more in control of your situation.*[22] But these traits are what will ultimately keep you alive. Foster them now and increase your chances of staying alive later.

The Ultimate Fighter: A Study in Mental Preparation

MMA and UFC fighters have a framework within their developmental process that incorporates the principal referred to as becoming an "elite purposeful performer." Mental Performance Specialist to athletes and Fightmedicine.Net contributor Will Lenzner describes a purposeful performer as "an individual whose renewed sense of self-improvement is triggered each and every day; a person whose thoughts and attitudes are driven solely by his or her commitment to their lifestyle." This is the same mental preparation demanded of the ultimate SAM. Lenzner asserts that one of the most crucial steps to becoming an elite purposeful performer is through mental preparation. In his article Improving MMA Performance with Mental Preparation he states:

---

22   Pennington, Tess, Are You Ready Series: Using Mental Preparedness to Survive, http://readynutrition. com/resources/are-you-ready-series-using-mental-preparedness-to-survive_26082013/

"*Preparation is the single most important ingredient to becoming a habitual purposeful performer, and champion. Simple preparation factors (having every item of your training gear, stretching, proper nutrition) are regarded as mere basics by elite purposeful performers. To truly reap the benefits of your training and maximize your competitive opportunities, you must be intensely committed to establishing behaviors that set you apart from your peers. Do you perform dynamic mental strengthening routines by reading or training your mental skills? These areas are essential to separating yourself from your peers.*

Three factors in your daily preparation must include: performance analysis, video feedback, and goal setting. Performance analysis involves setting a MISSION for each session, and reviewing your training after each session.

Mission

A mission is essentially a commitment to how you will perform. Notice it doesn't suggest how you might perform, or how you hope to perform? This is a declaration, a contract with you. You are affirming what you will do with a confident mind and conviction in your heart. I encourage my clients to use acronyms, quotations and mantras as their missions. They commonly use go-to lines, which stimulate desired mental and physical responses.

Training Review

When reviewing your training it can be helpful to examine each session using the W.I.L.L. format:

- *__W__ell—Focus on what you did well, the positives. Anchor those moments and allow them to become part of your muscle memory. Mentally rehearse them, and strengthen them by setting out to do them again.*

- *__I__mprove—Identify what you can improve upon. If you're uncomfortable or weak in a specific performance area, acc* *it as an opportunity to get better and set out to do just that.*

- *__L__earned __L__everage—Come away with tangible learning outcomes that you can leverage for the future. Examples most often include areas you learned about yourself in certain performance moments and proper technique execution.*

Elite purposeful performers are not created overnight. To become one, you must adjust your daily thoughts, attitudes and behaviors, and live by these standards every day. Separate yourself from others. Accept the challenge."[23]

Lenzner's ideas about an athlete's mental preparation translate well metaphorically in any profession, especially in sales. Success in any profession is equal to the preparation of your mind—your ability to find confidence and the drive to succeed—your drive to win.

Lessons From the Ultimate Sales Assassin Master:

1. Any survival situation requires a great deal of mental effort to keep you positive, relaxed and confident.

2. Figuratively and literally, get off the defense! Get rid of the defensive posture and get rid of the defensive attitude.

3. Remember, the Sales Assassin is always focused on the things you CAN control with the proper mindset:
   a. Your daily schedule of work
   b. Understanding your products and services
   c. Developing and implementing your sales strategy
   d. The individualized approach to each client
   e. Visualizing your engagement, your words and actions, in response to different scenarios

---

23   http://fightmedicine.net/mma-health/improving-mma-performance-with-mental-preparation

CHAPTER 4

SAM BELT 3: ESTABLISHING THE SALES ASSASSIN MINDSET

IN SAM BELT 2 Mental Preparation I state that becoming a SAM demands a mentally conditioned and prepared mind. Without it, it's literally impossible to be able to create the type of mental focus and discipline needed to achieve what we will discuss in this chapter called the Sales Assassin Mindset.

As sales professionals, our minds can be our greatest enemy. Without the proper mindset you will be doomed to failure. I am a person who has the tendency to act upon emotion and one of my most challenging quests in life has always been learning how to get and sustain control of my mindset. This is one of the most difficult tasks that you will have to master in order to change your direction in sales. Control your mindset and watch your net worth grow. Learn to control your mindset and you will be in control of your greatest asset.

I don't know how many times I've said to my oldest daughter as she was going through her fun-filled teenage years, "Kristen, you need an attitude adjustment." I'm an expert on this term because my mother gave me the same adjustment warning everyday of my teenage life and thank goodness she did. The real truth is we all need attitude adjustments at various points of our life. Our mental attitude dictates how we act and respond to and interpret various situations in our life. The problem we all have is that our attitudes get out of whack and can cause us all types of problems. However, our mental attitude can be a source of strength and positive performance, if we can master the ability to adjust and control it when necessary.

- How do your mental attitudes affect your personal and professional life?
- Where does your mental attitude come from?
- Does your attitude change day to day?
- What causes your mental attitude to change?

I am certainly no scholar of psychology, but I try to expose myself to as much as I can and learn from others. Carol Dweck, a Stanford University researcher on the concept of mindset said, *"I was obsessed with understanding how people cope with failures…"*[24] What the true SAM learns from Dweck's work is that we are each born with a certain level of intelligence and innate abilities. However, beyond this point we develop more knowledge and our habits, attitudes, ideas and ways of thinking are exposed. Our intelligence is just the starting point and will only get us so far. The rest is developed, molded and shaped through lessons of experience and life and most importantly through our dedication and drive to learn and succeed. The Sales Assassin Master knows this and feels it. **Mindset is your fixed mental attitude or disposition that predetermines your response to and interpretation of situations we face each day.**

24   Dweck, Carol S. PhD, 2006. Mindset, The New Psychology of Success, http://books.google.com/
     books?id=fT6U0Ee7_kQC&pg=PA3&lpg=PA3&dq="I+was+obsessed+with+understanding+
     how+people+cope+with+failures"&source=bl&ots=kFEIyAgZQi&sig=6UbpK2qLIvG5ctzeBFisOLWs
     g2o&hl=en&sa=X&ei=ELT2UpOmDsecyQH0yIDABg&ved=0CCoQ6AEwAQ—v=onepage&qh

***

Wisdom from Anthony Caliendo, the Ultimate Sales Assassin

The right mindset creates and paves the way to success. It motivates us and makes us more productive each day.

Mind Rollercoaster Phenomenon

A rollercoaster has a series of high peaks and low points so that when riding on one, we feel our most exhilarated when we're at the highest height! In sales, that's exactly the sensation we feel when we've just achieved a success, like scoring a meeting with a huge prospect and even further, finally closing that big deal that we've been working on forever. Yes, those kinds of highs are what drives us in sales and what keeps our passion and dedication alive!

The Mind Rollercoaster Phenomenon (MRP) is how I describe the mental state of a sales professional who allows certain occurrences, distractions or obstacles and negative thinking to deflect them from productivity. Almost every day, you are a dartboard which darts are being thrown at and some of them will hit the bulls-eye. In other words, you will face constant obstacles that can be deadly to success. It's how you handle the obstacles that set you apart from the rest.

You may not be able to change daily occurrences, but you most certainly can change the way you respond and react to them in order to encourage certain outcomes. Remember, a SAM has a flame that stays alive while the average salesperson struggles to keep the flame alive.

We've all heard the words "negativity breeds negativity." One of the most important things you can do to keep your flame alive is to not get drawn in to negative thoughts and especially negative people. I always tell myself that negativity is like the devil, it will take you to hell in the blink of an eye. You must learn that negative thoughts are your path to defeat. If you can develop that proper mindset, which includes the daily weeding out of negativity, you will be further on the path to becoming a SAM.

So what are the factors that contribute to MRP, how do we counteract them so that we can develop a SAM mindset? As a sales person, as a professional, as an individual, the disposition of your mindset does not begin when you wake up in the morning. Your daily mindset begins *when you go to bed the night before!* Consider this: when you wake up in the morning you wake up having the same things on your mind that you had when you went to sleep the night before, good or bad. Those last thoughts and ideas you had on your mind right before you went to bed influence your disposition and your mindset within seconds of when your eyes open the next morning.

In "Marriage and Relationships 101" you learn, "never go to bed angry with your spouse." Why? It's because if you go to bed with unresolved issues and anger, you're going to wake up with the same unresolved issues, but with anger that was allowed to fester and stew overnight. Then what occurs? You wake up with those same unresolved issues and maybe a little resentment that you will, no doubt, carry with you for the rest of the day. These are feelings that affect you adversely for the remainder of your day. This same premise applies to learning how to control your mindset as it relates to your productivity at work. If you constantly begin your day on a low, it stands to reason that you will go through your day on a low, and constantly end your day on a low... and the vicious cycle continues.

Combating the Vicious MRP "Low-Low" Cycle

First and above all else, becoming a SAM means STOPPING the MRP; this vicious "low-low" cycle so you can gain control of your mindset—mastering your mind and having *exclusive* rights over your disposition. Cliché or not, "every day has to be a new day!" This is something that we declare out loud at my company, especially after having dealt with a contentious distraction. My business manager or I will say, "Well...tomorrow's a new day." If something occurs on a Friday, I'll say "Monday is a new day." This is one of the ways we train our minds to put distractions into perspective so that they do not interrupt our focus on our other goals. Creating an optimistic mindset means putting the negatives into perspective by clearing your mind and re-focusing on what you need to accomplish and achieve, and it begins when you go to bed at night. It sounds like a contradiction, but you actually have to learn how to wind down and gear up at the same time! Game plan mode essentially begins when you close your eyes at night. You must put this principle into immediate practice and BELIEVE IT if you want to acquire the skill of controlling your mindset.

Controlling Constant Distractions

MMA fighters train incessantly. If they're serious about their success in the sport, physical training becomes a 9 to 5 life commitment. The fighter endures unyielding conditioning via rigorous practice sessions and rigid diet regimens. He completely transforms himself. If you are a SAM, think of yourself as an MMA fighter at work. You are a warrior—a relentless beast, never distracted, never deviating from goal—victory and success.

Unfortunately, sales people are often easily distracted, which contributes to MRP. Perhaps too often, sales professionals are afforded the luxury of self-managing their professional lives, simply because of the nature of their jobs. They often work remotely from a home office and/or unsupervised. However, that flexibility sometimes easily allows for distraction.

As a matter of fact, there are way too many distractions on a daily basis that cause you not to produce. Let's think of them as falling into these categories:

1. **Personal distractions**—getting a call from a spouse regarding the house or finances, an issue at school with one of the children, or a friend needing advice.

2. **Business distractions**—a client issue, production or logistics issues, being reprimanded by a manager or long drawn out sales meetings, policy or commission changes.

3. **Self-imposed distractions**—iPhones, Facebook, Twitter, Instagram, Keeping Up with the Kardashians, etc.

So, with this immense propensity for distractions—personal, business, self-induced, avoidable or unavoidable—what if you could train your mind to think and react differently to distractions so as to mitigate loss of focus on daily production goals? It is absolutely possible and a requirement for success.

But let's go further. In order for you to effectively manage the distractions, you must first identify:

1. Which types of distractions consume you each day?

2. How do you react to your distractions?

3. Are your distractions real or are they *perceived?*

Exercise

For one full 5 day work week, identify, write down on a piece of paper, and carefully examine any and all occurrences during your work day that could be considered a distraction taking you out of your zone. Jot down how you reacted to them. Then categorize them business, personal, self-imposed. At the end of the 5 days, examine your list. Now you have some decisions to make.

Monday's Distractions:

1. Distraction 1:

   _____

   a. Personal   _____
   b. Professional   _____
   c. Self-imposed   _____

2. Distraction 2:

   _____

   a. Personal   _____
   b. Professional   _____
   c. Self-imposed   _____

3. Distraction 3:

   _____

    a. Personal _____

    b. Professional _____

    c. Self-imposed _____

Tuesday's Distractions:

1. Distraction 1:

_____

    a. Personal _____

    b. Professional _____

    c. Self-imposed _____

2. Distraction 2:

_____

    a. Personal _____

    b. Professional _____

    c. Self-imposed _____

3. Distraction 3:

_____

    a. Personal _____

    b. Professional _____

    c. Self-imposed _____

Wednesday's Distractions:

1. Distraction 1:

_____

   a. Personal   _____

   b. Professional   _____

   c. Self-imposed   _____

2. Distraction 2:

   _____

   a. Personal   _____

   b. Professional   _____

   c. Self-imposed   _____

3. Distraction 3:

   _____

   a. Personal   _____

   b. Professional   _____

   c. Self-imposed   _____

Thursday's Distractions:

1. Distraction 1:

   _____

   a. Personal   _____

   b. Professional   _____

   c. Self-imposed   _____

2. Distraction 2:

   _____

   a. Personal   _____

    b. Professional _____

    c. Self-imposed _____

3. Distraction 3:

_____

    a. Personal _____

    b. Professional _____

    c. Self-imposed _____

Friday's Distractions:

1. Distraction 1:

_____

    a. Personal _____

    b. Professional _____

    c. Self-imposed _____

2. Distraction 2:

_____

    a. Personal _____

    b. Professional _____

    c. Self-imposed _____

3. Distraction 3:

_____

    a. Personal _____

    b. Professional _____

    c. Self-imposed _____

If you're continually bombarded with personal distractions during your work day, the non-life threatening kind, accept and admit that these can be absolutely controlled and/or eliminated. Have the conversations you need to have with sources of your personal distractions! This also applies to self-imposed distractions. Unless you are a social media marketer by profession, then your non-business related Twitter feed is not more important than your productivity. If it is, then you need to re-evaluate your priorities!

If you have too many business distractions in a week, then you need to evaluate the importance and impact of these types of distractions. Can they be delegated to others to handle? Can they be addressed once without unnecessary escalation? Figure out how to mitigate business distractions by dealing only with those that are within your scope of responsibility. Get rid of the rest of them, if possible. Sometimes, they are unavoidable, you can't stop them. Just learn how to manage them.

Most important, after you evaluate your list, you need to figure out if your distractions are *real or perceived.* If there's one thing I know about sales people is that they are a melodramatic, sensitive and easily distracted breed. When the "shit hits the fan," the cell phones come out accompanied by wild pacing and profanity laced language. I know it, I live it! If it invokes reaction, it's usually "overreaction." So let me ask you again, are your distractions real or perceived? Or are they simply excuses? In other words, are you constantly, consciously (or unconsciously) giving yourself an out in order to avoid facing your sales production goals? This is important to think about and keep it real with yourself.

In order to develop a SAM mindset you must create a distraction barrier by doing the following things:

1. Determine if your distractions are real or perceived

2. Control them by figuring out how to appropriately address them. If it's personal, save it for after hours. If it's business, figure out a way to mitigate them

3. Practice the art of "closing your door and putting your blinders on"

Preventing the MRP "Idle Mind Syndrome"

On the other side of the spectrum, there is such a thing as an idle minded sales person, one with no action and no trigger. An idle mind is the Mind Rollercoaster Phenomenon's playground. If you fall into this category then you're simply not putting in the effort to build momentum and a pipeline. You need to put consistent energy into building activity and keeping your mind moving forward. Being too laid back without having a proactive mindset is a productivity killer! SAM achievement is a full-time discipline. There are times when it requires 12 hour days. Therefore, get yourself stimulated on a daily basis or else you'll have zero mindset!

MRP "Chasing the Clock Syndrome"

In life there are various types of clocks that influence our behaviors and our lives; the physical clock, the mental clock, the biological clock, etc. It seems that we're always cognizant of time ticking away, allowing us or hindering us from completing the tasks and achieving the goals that we've set forth for ourselves. Especially in today's fast paced, technology and device driven world where multi-tasking and cramming as much on our to-do lists as possible are the new normal. With that comes pressure to get it done and frustrations manifest themselves when the clock stops ticking and your time runs out.

***

Wisdom from Anthony Caliendo, the Ultimate Sales Assassin

My watch only tells me the time of day. It does not control me. I tell myself when I want to get things done. I must control me. This is my mindset.

How often do you find yourself saying "there's not enough hours in the day…" or "it's Friday and I haven't even looked at this project…" or even, "I can't believe it's already the end of the month and…" That's because you're constantly "chasing the clock," which essentially means you're in a suspended state of MRP because you're consistently NOT meeting whatever tasks or goals within the timeframe you've expected of yourself.

They say in life there are two constants: death and taxes. Well, in sales, the daily, weekly or monthly clock is as prevalent and unavoidable as death and taxes! If you are constantly chasing the clock, then your clock has become a colossal, grotesque, loud ticking "MRP," sitting on your desk, obstructing your view, a hindrance, and an adversary. The key to becoming a SAM means learning how to manage your clock and transforming it into a well-oiled instrument helping you to remain coordinated and on track to meet your objectives.

Sales 101 teaches the concept of proper time management, prioritizing, so on and so forth. However, the Ultimate SAM is here to teach you that as you're developing the mindset of a SAM, you are actually *fine tuning* your mental clock. I'm not, by any means, undermining the basics (i.e. writing down daily or weekly objectives or setting monthly targets and production quotas. These are key principles relating to goals and objectives). However, as a SAM you will learn how to manage the clock and rely upon your own mental awareness and instincts whereby you know that proper management of your daily tick-tock affects your weekly tick-tock, and affects your monthly clock. Your clock is your production success! Your biggest production successes occur when you've mastered the ability to control the tick-tock of the clock! Even further, becoming a SAM means that the clock no longer dominates you; it becomes a non-factor in every aspect of your life.

MRP: When there are not enough "highs" as there might be "lows"

We've previously defined the Mind Rollercoaster Phenomenon as the emotional ups and downs of business and personal life, distractions or aversions that affect your productivity. Remember a rollercoaster has a series of high peaks and low points so that when riding on one, we feel our most exhilarated when we're at the highest height!

In business and our personal lives, the challenge is dealing with the lows. What if there aren't as many highs as there are lows? In the world of sales, lows come in the form of rejection, non-response, non-results, non-activity, the "Ground Hog Day Syndrome" = lack of new business. The typical salesperson deals with lows by becoming de-motivated and dejected and going back to the cigar bar over a beer and sorting business card prospects. Let's go back to our rollercoaster analogy. When you're riding a roller-coaster and you're slowly approaching the top of a peak, you feel such a strong sense of anticipation. And when you've reached that highest point before taking the plunge, the exhilaration and elation are absolutely immense. Then the rollercoaster takes its plunge and while you are on that rapid descent...your hands in the air...waiving like you don't care...you feel totally invincible! Then, what happens? You have to ride out the low points until you're on track to another high. This is how a SAM responds to the lows in sales. You must have the SAM mindset that will allow you to focus on creating more highs while you're "riding out" the lows. The anticipation of ascending to another peak will encourage you and motivate you to achieve the next exhilarating high. A SAM does this by keeping his or her pipeline fresh and replenished, by living each day with the EXPECTATION that there will be another high. High-powered Ultimate SAMs can even ride multiple roller coasters at the same time. Having a SAM mindset dictates that one knows that the highs are for certain and the lows are merely pit stops on the way to your next high. Remember you are never going to be sure when the next high or low will occur...So Be Prepared!

Body and Physical Preparation

Experts agree there's no better way to put your mind and body into perfect synergy than with exercise and physical activity. On your journey to developing the proper mindset and to becoming a SAM, there's no better way to help build your will and desire to succeed than by integrating fitness goals into the game plan. An athlete knows he or she won't be great without the proper mindset. Most importantly, they know that the proper physical training will help develop his or her discipline and drive for success. Well, think of yourself as an athlete at work; better yet envision yourself as a SAM. Starting your morning with physical activity releases those endorphins and gives you the energy and "natural high" promoting the SAM mindset. Ending your day with physical activity helps clear your mind of the day's negative distractions, promotes restful REM sleep and helps you wind down and gear up for the next day.

The hit reality TV series "The Biggest Loser" is one of my absolute favorite shows. If you've never seen it, I encourage you to tune in. The show features extremely obese individuals who decide to make a commitment to losing the weight by adhering to a strict exercise and diet plan. As they go on their weight loss journey and begin reaching their weight loss goals, you see them begin to build energy, gain momentum, confidence and become more driven to succeed. They go to bed and rise every morning with the "every day is a new day" mindset and an opportunity to reach new milestones. Wow, imagine being able to apply that kind of excitement to your sales objectives. By incorporating fitness goals into your journey to becoming a SAM, you will become The Biggest Winner, I guarantee it! I'm not by any means suggesting that if you don't then you won't, but I submit to you that when you're in better physical health, you look better, you feel better and you're more confident. These positive feelings contribute to a positive disposition and a positive mindset. Because now you're getting your mind and body to work in unison, you're making better choices about what to feed your mind and about what to feed your body.

Coincidentally, physical fitness all begins with the mind. You have to train your mind to train your body to promote mental and physical fitness. All of this leads to the proper mindset for achieving goals in sales and in your life. Setting tangible, measurable goals works for fitness just as sales. Nike knows this: the new Nike FuelBand motivates you to measure, track and compare your fitness results with your friends: just as sales people compare and compete on sales goals. I love these types of tools and they work for me both professionally and personally.

Level Setting Your Mindset

Your mindset is your belief and attitude about yourself and your most basic qualities and capabilities. Think about your professional sales skills and your intelligence, your talents, your personality. Are these qualities fixed and forever carved in stone? Or are you willing to grow and cultivate yourself and mold and shape who you are and what you want to be? When you manage and control the Mind Rollercoaster Phenomenon, you know and feel that you are evolving each day through personal and professional dedication and your effort and desire for success. No, you may not be Tiger Woods, Michael Jordan, Steve Jobs, Jack Welch or Tony Robbins. But you can and must use the tools they used to achieve their greatness—the passion for success, the passion to practice and learn, the willingness to fail in order to succeed and the mindset to perceive the odds.

> *The Mindset Paradox: The greatest threat to success is avoiding failure.*
> *One of the most provocative aspects of Dweck's work is what it says about our approach to challenges. With a growth mindset, you focus on learning and development rather than failure and actively pursue the types of challenges that will likely lead to both learning and failure.*[25]

---

25 Dweck, Carol S. PhD, 2006. Mindset, The New Psychology of Success.

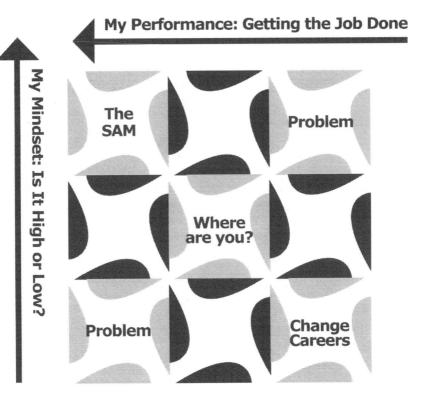

My Performance: Getting the Job Done

My Mindset: Is It High or Low?

The SAM

Problem

Where are you?

Problem

Change Careers

Lessons From the Ultimate Sales Assassin Master:

1. Mindset is your fixed mental attitude or disposition that predetermines your response to and interpretation of situations we face each day.

2. The right mindset creates and paves the way to success. It motivates us and makes us more productive each day.

3. The key to controlling your mindset is controlling your mental rollercoaster that distracts us from goals we set for ourselves.

Find the Balance
Mindset and Performance

The Ultimate Fighter: Finding Your Mindset

All successful athletes need "game," which simply means that they must possess the highest levels of drive, skill, instinct, physical prowess and desire to win in order to succeed. The recipe is a mixture of the outer-physical game and the inner-mental game, which fails to rise without all of the necessary ingredients.

In any professional capacity and particularly in sales, you have to have outer game. When you're meeting with a prospect, showing a house, or exhibiting at a tradeshow you have to have remarkable presence and a polished presentation or that first impression that you cannot make twice is all but lost. Sales people and athletes alike, especially boxers and MMA fighters, should work tirelessly on their outer game so that they can build that perception of strength, confidence, endurance, and physicality. However, without conditioning that inner game or the mindset, the outer game ceases to exist.

Fight fans or fans of any combative sport, do you ever take notice of a contender's demeanor before the match? There's a lot of mental posturing going on between the two opponents. Each fighter knows that they must harness as much mental and emotional intensity as possible before he or she meets in the center of the ring and each fighter has his or her own style and way of doing it. Some are hyped up and bloodthirsty, punching themselves in the head while others have a poker face determination with a deafening calm in his or her body and demeanor. Call it intimidation, call it psyching out your opponent, even if one of them already knows they are doomed, call it what you like. It's all a part of their inner game; the mindset and being in the zone.

Lessons From the Ultimate Sales Assassin Master:

1. Mindset is your fixed mental attitude or disposition that predetermines your response to and interpretation of situations we face each day.

2. Remember, you will face constant obstacles that can be deadly to success. It's how you handle the obstacles that set you apart from the rest.

3. The right mindset creates and paves the way to success. It motivates us and makes us more productive each day.

4. The key to controlling your mindset is controlling your mental rollercoaster that distracts you from goals you set for yourself.

5. You may not be able to change daily occurrences, but you most certainly can change the way you respond and react to them in order to encourage certain outcomes. Remember, a SAM has a flame that stays alive while the average salesperson struggles to keep the flame alive.

CHAPTER 5

SAM BELT 4:
GOAL SETTING AND ACHIEVEMENT

The reason most people never reach their goals is that they don't define them, learn about them or even seriously consider them as believable or achievable. Winners can tell you where they are going, what they plan to do along the way, and who will be sharing the adventure with them.[26]
—Denis Waitley

***

THE ABILITY TO set the proper goals and then have the ability to achieve these goals is not the easiest task for anyone and certainly not for sales professionals. No one can achieve greatness in all levels of their life. But to have any shot at success you first have to know what you want to achieve and then have a plan to achieve it.

Sales executives, their management teams and sales professionals annually set sales goals for their teams. This is a very difficult process for most people, especially understanding the importance of achieving buy-in at all levels on the reasonableness of those goals. To most professionals they hear a certain bottom-line message, *"sell more than you did last year."* Unfortunately for most people

---

26   Waitley, Denis. The Motivation Speakers Hall of Fame, http://getmotivation.com/dwaitley.htm

it doesn't matter what process the organization goes through to "negotiate" goals and it doesn't matter if you call it a collaborative effort based upon a tried and tested formula, it still comes down to most professionals as "get out there and sell more than you did last year." It's very unfortunate that most managers have yet to understand the process as anything more than a demand for more sales. More important is for managers to have a deeper conversation after defining goals. This conversation is focused on how your goals are going to be achieved.

Let's Talk Sports

Athletes and coaches succeed by creating big goals—win the championship this year. But their big goals can only be achieved by accomplishing a series of small goals—win one game, practice 6 days a week—2 hours per day, average 400 offensive yards per game, average 0 turnovers per game, maintain a 70% free throw average, keep the team healthy.

***

Wisdom from Anthony Caliendo, the Ultimate Sales Assassin

The Formula = Think Really Big, But Start Small, One Day At A Time, One Win At A Time

In sports an athlete is driven to win the game, the match, the series, the Super Bowl, NBA Championship, The National Championship. It's the end result. It's the final achievement. It is the goal.

What athletes realize is that it takes a series of small goals and accomplishments to achieve the big prize or the ultimate goal of winning the match or championship. In other words, the big prize or ultimate goal cannot be achieved without preparation or achieving a series of smaller goals that build as a foundation to greater success. And that along with achieving the smaller goals, there will be failures. What are these small intermediate goals that athletes work to achieve that lead to the big prize?

- The daily goals around practice repetition
- The daily goals around a practice routine
- The goal to score points
- The goal of making first downs
- The goal of excelling in rank to become the #1 contender
- A field goal kicker will not end practice without making a series of field goals from each length up to 50 yards
- A running back will have a personal goal of achieving a minimum of 4 yards each time he carries the ball
- A tennis player will not stop a practice session until he makes 20 perfect serves without a fault
- An MMA fighter will complete four consecutive full days of intense training consisting of cardio, strength training, sparring and ground routines to perfect his game

These intermediate goals work toward minimizing error and maximizing success. Working on these goals allows them to be more confident and builds on the ultimate goals of winning each game and ultimately winning the championship or the title.

The Sales Assassin thinks the same way. I was meeting with a young man who was just starting out as a real estate agent. He was sitting at the bar of my local cigar joint jabbing at his tablet, puffing away and mumbling to himself. He was only a few months into his new career and already frustrated and depressed. He had just spent about 30 days on a deal that crashed to a screeching halt when the client didn't qualify for the mortgage. He spent the next 15 minutes whining about everything he did to get the deal and then it fell through. I said to him, "Bro, you're whining about things that you can't control. Let's back up and discuss your goals. You've been in this new job for a couple months and at the first sign of things not going well, you're ready to throw in the towel."

This new sales guy's head was full of new information, however what he had not realized is the only path to success was to put this new information in a form that would drive him to success. As we have already said, "The ability to sell is the ability to learn." But further, it is the ability to apply the things we learn into an orderly framework that will guide you. You have to be willing to change how you think and how you behave and use the new techniques. New techniques take practice and practice is about repetition. We do repetitions to change our previous behavior. My next challenge to the young man was simple, "Let's start over and put all this information you have in front of you together in a fashion you can understand, starting with some goals and layout a plan to achieve your goals."

Another way to think about goals is deciding how you are planning your future performance. This is exactly what an athlete does. They plan and establish goals to drive future performance. Planning for your sales performance is designed to keep you from wandering aimlessly from day to day and year to year, without focusing on what you want to achieve and need to achieve.

We all have hopes and dreams for the future, and in our mind define goals or some type of plan to achieve success. However, most people ponder the big decisions and goals in our lives, but tend to ignore smaller goals/issues that tend to drive and support the bigger picture. We must realize that our attitudes and gut instincts tend to guide the smaller issues that matter in your sales career. The SAM succeeds from an organized approach each day to determine what you want to achieve, remembering that it's the details that get us to and through the big goals .

> *"If you can dream it, you can achieve it.[27]"*
> —Zig Ziglar

***

Choose SMARTS Goals: The concept of defining SMARTS goals is not new to business, but sales professionals and many sales leaders' goals have no logical pattern for development of what needs to be achieved. Goals must be a basis for what you need to do each day for success. Ryan Blair, a well-known American entrepreneur, author and specialist on achieving goals, tells us, *"Focus creates a powerful force: goal power. The moment you focus on a goal, your goal becomes a magnet, pulling you and your resources toward it. The more focused your energies, the more power you generate."*[28] This is the heart of the best sales professional's success. Establishing the right goals, finding the right plan to achieve the goals and then executing that plan reaps tremendous rewards.

Many sales pros are struggling daily, treading the deep sea of potential failure, and barely keeping their head above water. They

---

27   Ziglar. http://www.ziglar.com/quotes/if-you-can-dream-it-you-can-achieve-it
28   Gary Ryan Blair. http://www.garyryanblair.com, Goals: The 10 Rules for Achieving Success.

find themselves in a business rut, working in a business instead of working on the business and controlling the business. Generally, you know what you need to be working on, but there are only 24 hours in the day, and you don't know how to develop a strategy or the path to success. The result is you just keep treading water, praying for the miracle payday. Is this your life? If it is, then SMARTS goal setting will give you an action plan to grow your business, not just a "get more sales" mentality.

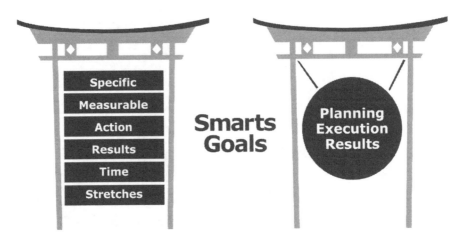

SAM Goal Development Process or Establish SMARTS Goals for Success

SMARTS Goals Defined

SPECIFIC: Your SAM goals must first be specific. When goals are specific, they have a much greater chance of being accomplished. You must decide the specific reasons, purposes or benefits of accomplishing the goal. Obviously, when working within a company setting it is important to negotiate all elements of the goals. The bottom line is simply that your goals should clearly and specifically define what you want to accomplish.

Example: A non-specific general goal would be, "Lose Weight."

But to make this goal specific you would say, "lose 50 pounds this year by going on a diet."

As a SAM, a specific goal would be to sell $50,000 worth of product this year through development of new customers in the South Florida region.

MEASURABLE: Your SAM goals contain specific, concrete criteria for measuring progress toward the attainment of each goal you set. When your progress is measureable, you know when you are on track to reach your target dates, dollar amounts or other criteria. When achieving these incremental measures, it's an opportunity to celebrate and feel the exhilaration of achievement that spurs you on to continue the effort required to reaching your ultimate goal.

To determine if your goals are measurable, here is a series of questions that the measure should answer:

1. How much?
2. How many?
3. How will I know when it is accomplished?
4. Does the measure give me a message on my progress?

Example: A non-specific general goal would be, "Lose Weight." But to make this goal measurable you would say, "lose 50 pounds this year by going on a diet and starting an exercise program that supports me **losing an average of 1 to 2 pounds per week**." As a SAM, a specific, measurable sales goal would say to sell $50,000 worth of product this year by development of new customers in the south Florida region, **acquiring an average of 2 new customers per month and averaging a minimum of $2,000 in sales for each new client.**

ATTAINABLE: Setting goals is important, but if you don't have a reasonable chance to attain these goals you are going to be frustrated. Goals have to be attainable. I often express concerns to companies when their sales quotas for the sales force are a reflection of their frustration with the performance of the company. Face it sales managers: setting unattainable goals is not going to rescue the overall company performance. When goals are attainable, sales people begin to more quickly discover ways to achieve success. They develop the habits, attitudes, beliefs, abilities, skills, and financial capacity to reach their goals. They are then able to see opportunities to inch closer to success.

When a SAM can see the ability to achieve success, you build your self-image and your self-confidence. You can feel success and feel worthy of the goals you have set. It's at that point that the swagger in your walk and your talk becomes a part of you. It's at this point that you are feeling confident in your plan and you will take the smart and wise steps forward. You can attain almost any goal you set when you plan your steps wisely and establish a time frame that allows you to carry out those steps. Goals that may have seemed far away and out of reach eventually move closer and become attainable, not because your goals shrink, but because you grow and expand to match them.

> *"Success is a state of mind. If you want success start thinking of yourself as a success."*[29]
> —Dr. Joyce Brothers

***

REALISTIC: To be realistic, a goal must be doable. This doesn't

---

29   Dr. Joyce Brothers. http://www.biography.com/people/joyce-brothers-21224553

mean the goal is easy, but it represents targets that you can see the end of and are willing, able and desire to work toward. The goal makes sense in our mind and we know we can reach the top.

Defining realistic goals is a learning process and learning curve. You have the capabilities to gain traction in your effort to support the strategy and goals of the organization for which you work. Realistic goals push you inside and outside, but they should not break your drive and spirit to achieve success. Finally, when goals are realistic you can realistically ask yourself if you have accomplished anything similar in the past and determine what were the conditions that allowed your success.

Example: Is it realistic that a 300 lb. offensive lineman can achieve a goal to condition his body to run a forty-yard dash in 4.5 seconds? Probably not. But it may be realistic that the lineman can improve and achieve a goal of increasing his speed to 4.8 seconds from 5.0 seconds. For a new sales person it may not be realistic to achieve the same sales goals as the professional who has been working in the field for 5 years and has an established territory.

Take into consideration several key points:

- Setting realistic, stretch goals requires a plan or a way of achieving success

- The goal needs to be realistic for you and where you are at that moment in your life and your career

- Be sure to set goals that you can attain yet take significant effort

- If the goal is too difficult and unrealistic, you may be setting a course for failure

- If the goal is too easy it sends the message that you aren't very capable of achieving success

Let's be clear, a goal can be very high and yet realistic. You must understand your limits and be able to determine that every goal represents an effort and that you can make substantial progress. Also, these goals should not be too low or too easy. The way the mind and body works is that goals that are really low demand less of us and demand less of our potential. You can't improve if things are too easy. A SAM would never be content with a set of goals that are a cakewalk to achieve. A SAM wants to run like a thoroughbred, always ready for the challenge. When they are successful, they feel it. Hard work becomes a goal and success is a labor of our love for what we do and the passion we have doing the job well.

TIME-BOUND: SAM goals must contain a timetable for goal achievement. The timetable established provides you the sense of urgency that will drive your performance. Time-bound is the simplest of the SMARTS criteria. Let's say your sales goals are calculated monthly and your goal is to hit $100,000 per month in production. You would manage your overall goal by breaking it down into 4 target weeks. In this example, your weekly target in sales production is $25,000. Ideally, you would strive to hit your production target each week. However, for each week that you don't hit your target you'd have to carry over to the next week the amount you were unable to hit the week prior. The higher figure you carry over, the harder you have to work in order to achieve your monthly goal.

Example: If your goal is to lose 30 lbs., the question is simple: by when do you want to lose 30 lbs.? Be assured, losing 30 lbs. without a timetable isn't going to cut it—you probably won't lose anything and will probably gain more weight. The key to placing a timeframe on your goals is driving your mind to automatically kick into gear to support the goal.

STRETCHES YOU: It was GE's Jack Welch who coined the concept that goals must stretch our capabilities. Yes, the best goals are those that stretch our mental and physical sales capabilities. Goals aren't supposed to be easy. Welch differentiated the concept of stretch goals by simply saying if goals can be easily achieved then why should we bother?

***

"By reaching for what appears to be the impossible, we often actually do the impossible. And even when we do not quite make it, we inevitably wind up doing much better than we would have done."[30]
—Jack Welch

Welch realized that it is not the company itself or the financial issues that drive success. Stretch goals exist no matter what the company's economic conditions. He felt that it was the sum total of stretch goals each individual achieves that makes the difference in company success. The economic environment, good or bad, has no impact on the purpose of setting stretch goals.

A SAM believes that stretching yourself pushes you to think in a different way about achieving success. My philosophy is that sales people have been stuck in the traditional thought process of believing that sales goals are simply achieved by calling everyone in

---

30   Collier, Nathan S., 2011. Stretch Goals, http://www.nscblog.com/miscellaneous/stretch-goals/

your address book. The SAM way is to stretch your mind to think differently about how and what customers and potential customers think about you, your products and services. The question isn't about finding the way to make money or growing share of market, but instead think about the task of sales in a new or different way— find new and innovative ways to work. A SAM believes that stretch goals require you to leverage the knowledge, skills, and abilities of others. More importantly, you must strive to appreciate that you are not an island of knowledge and you need advice and counsel from others for success.

Questions Beyond the Goals

Understanding how to develop great goals is step one, but your success demands not only a further look into each goal in terms of planning, but a tenacious "kick-ass" approach to getting the necessary work done. Whether you are acting in a sales leadership capacity or facilitating your own sales or business goals, you must take the time to ask and address several vital questions:

Do you have a strategy to achieve each goal or do you assume it will come together?

What is the value proposition that you are offering, communicating and driving?
Why should anyone you're selling to care?
Why should they want your product?
Why should they want to buy from you?

What are going to be the clear barriers to your success? Are you ready for them when they raise their ugly heads?

Are your sales goals dependent on other people getting their job done? If you are dependent on others how are you going to anticipate the potential problems with these individuals?

How are you going deal with the competition?
How are you going to offset what they are offering?
They aren't going to go away just because you want them to.

5 Questions for the Sales Professional

5 Questions For Sales Leadership

If you are in a sales leadership position, you also have to ask yourself a series of questions that are designed to determine how you support your sales force goals:

1 Are you sure your sales professional has bought into their goals? Do you care that they have bought into the goals? Do they have the level of confidence necessary to achieve the goals?

2 Are you ready to assist them in addressing roadblocks that may sabotage goal attainment?

3 What is going to be your role in supporting the sales professional's goal achievements? How does the sales professional want and need to be supported around their goals?

4 How will you hold your sales professional accountable around reaching their goals and how will you engage them when progress against goals begins to flounder?

5 If you were in the sales professional's shoes, could you attain these goals? If yes, what would you be doing differently? Have you given the sales person your advice and counsel?

5 Questions For Sales Leadership

***

Wisdom from Anthony Caliendo, the Ultimate Sales Assassin

SAM exhilaration is the ability to achieve success by setting your goals high enough for satisfying achievement!

Case Study: Best Sales Assassin Practices At Work

Giovanni Capra, President of SynTec Corporation, has an important message for all sales force leaders, *"I tell all my sales people that I have never heard of a company that is successful by maintaining the status quo. You have to invest in the development of your sales force's understanding of the basic premise of sales work. The difference in success is the company who assists sales professionals to reach beyond the status quo and helps the sales force reach its potential and then stretch beyond the status quo. Goal establishment and management is an imperative. We believe in stretch goals that drive the business and drive individual sales professionals. Of course, financial goals drive our incentive opportunity, but there are small goals for each element of client interaction.*

We keep the process simple and we want all of our sales people to clearly understand several simple principals:

You will have the opportunity for success because we negotiate sales goals that present an opportunity for success.

Your sales goals are realistic, but we will stretch you to go beyond what is comfortable to achieve, but with the right effort, planning and support you can reach the stretch.

We also expect each sales professional to have documented goals to drive customers through the opportunity, leading to negotiation, then to the close process.

We need to have an ongoing communication with the sales force individually and collectively to make sure they have the knowledge, skills, abilities, and tools needed to understand and achieve the stretch goals.

On a weekly basis we meet with the sales force individually and collectively to understand the barriers to success and to answer questions and to challenge sales professionals to achieve their potential.

Each time we meet we refer to the tools and measures of success, continuously categorizing and qualifying potential customers to what we refer to as "Operational and Individual Revenue Streams".

We have learned that the most effective sales professionals need simple tools that simply motivate success. However, planning is always key. This is a learning process. Remember:

1. *Define the Opportunities*
2. *Convert Opportunities to Leads*
3. *Convert Leads to a Negotiation*
4. *Convert Negotiation to Closures*
5. *Closures Convert to Revenue*
6. *Revenue Converts to Money in Your Pocket*

The challenge we have and always strive to overcome is to teach sales professionals the difference in opportunities and leads. People have to understand that an opportunity is finding a favorable circumstance, person or company that has short, long term or future potential. An opportunity is a chance or prospect that has "opportunity or potential" to turn into a lead. A lead is the next step in the process. It's a progression and step in the process.

The best way to describe a lead is thinking in terms of establishing a relationship that has progressed to the point that you are figuratively taking them by the hand and leading them to a new place, with new ideas, new thoughts and new potential. We spend a significant amount of time each week in differentiating opportunities versus leads. When I interview sales candidates, they are often confused about these concepts. They will ask, "Will you provide me sales leads?" My response is always no, we will provide you opportunities. Your job is to convert an opportunity into a lead, that's what great sales professionals learn to do. Many organizations get these items confused, you must remember that opportunities turn into leads, leads turn into negotiations and negotiations turn into closing deals.

Giovanni Capra

President, SynTec Corporation

Key Points Around Goal Setting:

1. **Control Your Mindset:** As previously discussed, your mind controls and drives both your enthusiasm and your ability.

2. **Devise a plan around your goals:** Planning is key to all sales success and can make your goals become accomplishments. If you chose not to plan, then you chose not to be successful.

   a. **Clearly define your goals in writing and include complete details:**

      i. Timetable for milestones

      ii. Any cost that might be associated with the goal

      iii. Define who, what, when, where, how

      iv. Resources required

      v. Rewards for achieving goals

3. **Stick With Your Plan, Yet Stay Flexible:** You have to develop and stick with your plan and work to overcome obstacles that will take you off task. Do not procrastinate. Make yourself accountable to others. If possible, be accountable to others beyond your boss. Be accountable to your customers. Agree

on deadlines and tell them to feel free to remind you of your commitments. The plan also needs to be flexible so you can adjust it as you progress. There is an old saying that states, "Plans are created and designed to change," as the situation and circumstances progress.

4. **Reassess:** Being flexible means being willing to reassess your needs and those of the client. As a Sales Assassin you will regularly re-examine your goals to ensure you are on track. The ability to reassess also allows you to recognize and celebrate the successes. Adaptation to new situations and circumstances is necessary, yet it allows you to stay on track to your key goal. Work hard and stay focused on the result.

5. **Establish Priorities:** Establishing priorities are part of the SAM way of life. Being able and willing to set priorities makes you better prepared to define your goals, and manage your pressure and anxiety levels more effectively. As stress increases, we are often forced to prioritize our commitments and decide which things can be put to one side and which can't.

Lessons From the Ultimate Sales Assassin Master:

1. Continually achieving higher status and upward mobility means setting goals and outlining strategic plans for consistent achievement. The only way to gauge your success is by setting goals, tracking measurable progress, and observing successes when goals have been realized. Trying to build success without having measurable, attainable goals is like running a race without a finish line!

2. Set two sets of goals: "Target" goals and "Challenge" goals.

3. Whatever attainable goals that you set for yourself, achieve them.

4. Without a strategic plan in place designed to help you reach your goals your chances of achieving them are slim to none.

Goal Planning Worksheet

Goal			
Time-Table for Completion			
SMARTS Checklist	☐ Specific ☐ Measureable ☐ Achievable ☐ Results Oriented ☐ Time-Bound ☐ Stretches Me		

Tasks Required for Success

Tasks Necessary to Achieve Goals	Due Date	Track Barriers and Results
Task 1:		
Task 2:		
Task 3:		
Task 4:		
Task 5:		

Anthony Caliendo, The Sales Assassin in His Domain

Dairy Foods Magazine Cover Story with Mary Beth Tomasino, CEO of JVM Sales Corp

My First Cousin, Frank Caliendo, Comedian and Impressionist with the "Chicago Boys"

Arnold Schwarzenegger Classic with Margret Ceja and Anthony Caliendo

The Frank Caliendo Show, Las Vegas

Joey Fatone and Anthony at 560 WQAM Radio, South Beach

Boca Life
M A G A Z I N E

ANTHONY CALIENDO
Against The Odds

PROFILE
By David Wilkening

When Delray Beach businessman Anthony Caliendo ran into Dan, Marino one night at trendy Nikki Beach Miami, the former Miami Dolphins quarterback put on his familiar lopsided grin. "Anthony, you're the Main Man," he said. After Caliendo greeted him back, Marino added: "Listen, just remember, you may be the main man, but I'm Dan the Man."

Running into celebrities he knows is nothing new for Caliendo, who says factually without boasting that he may know more celebrities than anyone in the area ("I can't tell you how many celebrities I know"). But the man who worked for years with another super-celebrity, Arnold Schwarzenegger, dismisses this as being a far less import3nt quality than others.

"Knowing celebrities has nothing to do with being a good businessman, " he says. What does help is working hard at it, and who works for you. "The secret to success is the team, who you have working for you. That's really what makes or breaks you." he says.

Caliendo, known as an incredible marketing machine, is famous for his "Main Man" media ads and talk show appearances that get his 'face in front of his clientele, weighted heavily toward 35- to 55-year-old men.

This explains Caliendo's wide acquaintance with sports, and the media activities associated with it The "Main Man" name was even associated with sports: it was how a sports radio talk show host introduced Caliendo, and he took it as an advertising motto.

He certainly has an ego, but he also has a sense of humor. An associate says Caliendo decorates his office with gongs, swords and gangster-like pictures of himself.

As Caliendo tells it, he started out the seventh child in humble circumstances in South Florida. He grew up without the support of a father and was raised by a single mother.

He still recalls the advice of his grandfather who told him in the seventh grade he should go out and get a job.

"I didn't grow up in a college-educated family, so my grandfather asked me what I was doing. I told

him school. He said I was going to be broke unless I got a job. Can you imagine someone telling a 12-year-old kid that?"

Caliendo did not go to college but did start working early. At the age of 18, he became the youngest manager to oversee the Chicago Health & Tennis Gyms. A few years later, he spent three years building World Gyms with the bodybuilding movie star now known in California as the "Gubernator," a take-off on the Terminator films.

In his personal life, Caliendo is partial to cigars and family gatherings. He has seven children, ranging from an infant to grown stepsons. His 7-year-old son Anthony looks so much like the short but muscle-heavy Caliendo ("He's the spitting image") that he's known as the "main man junior."

He also devotes his time to charity

and fund raising, particularly for Kids in Distress, which deals with neglected and abused children in South Florida.

Most of his time away from work, however, finds him with his own seven children. One of their favorite activities is a drive through Lion County Safari followed by a visit to the beach for pizza and ice cream.

Caliendo's mortgage business in 2005 did $83 million in loan volume. The "Main Man" branched out recently into the real estate business. He also has plans to further expand his mortgage business.

The "Main Man" in mortgage today... but who knows where else tomorrow?

Photography By
TRACIE VAN AUKEN

Feature Story Boca Life Magazine: Against All Odds

Super Bowl XL ESPN 760 Radio Event with
Radio Personality Evan Cohen and Anthony

Anthony's work with "Kids in Distress", an organization dedicated to
the care and treatment of abused and neglected children, has been a
meaningful part of his life.

THE "Main Man" MAKES
THE HOLIDAYS SPECIAL
FOR CHILDREN IN NEED

Anthony Caliendo, better know as the "Main Man" in his numerous locally aired radio and television commercials, made the holidays a little merrier when he and his company, Acceptance Capital Mortgage, underwrote the annual Kids In Distress Palm Beach County Holiday Party for Foster Care families. Food, fun, and entertainment greeted more 50 families who attended the event in December at Delray Beach's Lake Ida Park.

"What a tremendous way to brighten the children's spirits," said Ellyn Okrent, Kids In Distress Executive Vice President." And it provided a tremendous opportunity for the foster care families to be able to network and provide support for another."

Kids In Distress was founded in Broward County in 1978 and has been providing foster care services in Palm Beach County since 2003. Currently, the organization supports over 100 foster homes in Palm Beach County.

Throughout 2005, Mr. Caliendo, Regional Manager of Delray Beach based Acceptance Capital Mortgage, has supported the work of Kids In Distress. Along with regular contributions to the organization from the profits made from completed mortgage contracts, he made his birthday party a fund-raiser as well as brought 40 children, who are being sheltered on Kids In Distress' Wilton manors campus to a recent Miami Heat basketball game.

"Kids In Distress is about strengthening families," said Mr. Caliendo. "With six kids of my own, I know how important that is to make a better tomorrow for all children and the community."

Child abuse is the nation's leading cause of death for children under three with more than three million cases of abuse reported each year. It's certainly a reality in Florida, where at least one of every 27 children in Florida is abused or neglected each year.

Kids In Distress recognizes that each child is different and each situation is different. But kids always come first and every decision made is based on the best interest of each child. When possible, children remain with their families. At Kids In Distress, there is support and structure for children and their families with the goal of achieving positive, lasting results.

Kids In Distress is committed to the highest standard of services, providing care and treatment in a safe environment, responding to the needs of the community and always striving for excellence.

For more than 25 years, Kids In Distress has demonstrated record of restoring abused and neglected children back to health through a well-integrated system of care that includes partnerships with community experts to meet the complex needs of children and their families, as well as a full continuum of care that includes therapeutic, shelter and group home care, and prevention, foster and adoption services. At Kids In Distress there is an entrepreneurial spirit where innovative programs are continually developed for children and their families. Last year alone, Kids In Distress provided assistance to more than 6,000 children and their families in South Florida.

For more information about Kids In Distress, call 561-272-9619 or visit www.kidsindistress.org.

Anthony's First Annual Kids In Distress Holiday Event for Foster Families

Celebrity cruise raises money for Kids In Distress

Anthony Caliendo left, and Tim Hardaway

Kids In Distress will, benefit from "The Main Man" event, a birthday celebration for Anthony Caliendo, regional director of Florida for Acceptance Capital Mortgage.

The celebration will take place during a celebrity cruise aboard First Lady", Yacht this Saturday from 6 to 10 p.m. Former Miami Heat, star Tim Hardaway will be the host.

With docking at the Westin Diplomat in " Hollywood, the evening's festivities will include a buffet dinner, entertainment, a silent auction and a raffle.

This fundraising celebrity cruise is just the latest way Caliendo has supported Kids In Distress. Recently, the mortgage company began donating portions of all receipts from closed mortgages to the agency.

For more than 25 years, Kids in Distress has had a demonstrated record of restoring abused and neglected children back to health through a full continuum of care that includes therapeutic, shelter and group home care, as well as , prevention, foster and adoption services.

Last year alone, Kids In Distress provided assistance to nearly 5,000 children and their families.

Ticket prices for the celebrity cruise range from $100 to $500.

For more information or to purchase tickets, e-mail events@kidsindistress.org.

Sun-Sentinel

The Main Man Birthday Bash benefiting Kids In Distress with Tim Hardaway and a cast of celebrities

Anthony Caliendo and Shaq

Anthony and Sir Lawrence Taylor

Anthony and Renowned Racer Danica Patrick at Indy 300

Golfing with Broadway Joe and the Guys at ESPN 106.3FM

Anthony and Phil Caliendo and Cousin Frank, the Comedian

CHAPTER 6

SAM BELT 5:
CLIENT QUALIFICATION PROCESS

CLIENT QUALIFICATION—THE MOST over used, abused, ignored, misunderstood and yet most valuable and indispensable tool of the sales process. Bottom-line, either learn to use it or definitely lose every great sales opportunity you will ever have.

Before the onslaught of the Internet world, sales professionals put every ounce of their effort into every sales meeting on their calendar. Every meeting was seen as the potential big sale opportunity. Online access to information and the new sales attitude has changed everything, paving the way to immediately and accurately weigh which leads are worth your efforts and which ones are not worth your time. Every sales professional must learn the modern concept of properly qualifying each sales lead. This skill will be the difference between landing a rich new business deal and wasting lots of time, energy and money, barking up the wrong tree. Your time is money! An efficient, effective qualification process saves time and increases your revenue!

*A 5% increase in selling time can yield a 20% increase in revenue,
a 1% increase in pipeline value can yield a 25% increase in
revenue, and a 15% decrease in the length of the sales cycle can
yield a 30% increase in revenue.[31]*
—Jon Miller

> CMO Institute named Jon a Top 10
> CMO for companies under $250
> million revenue

Could there be a profession that hangs on optimism any more than sales? In fact, the entire profession from the CEO to sales management to the front-line sales professional exists on optimism. Even the best SAM is hard-wired for eternal hope and an optimistic view that tomorrow the big contract will be signed. This hope is grounded in the organization's faith in one of a number of sales qualification methodologies. No one methodology offers the perfect formula for success, yet each is designed to increase your effectiveness and drive revenue. The greatest problem and challenge to each of these qualification methods is how they are implemented. Sales qualification discussions are the greatest source of controversy in the sales industry. Despite the debates, it is the execution of the methodology that differentiates the most successful organization. What I do know is that the sales qualification method that is too complex and laden with jargon can impede the sales process. The method that is not technical or precise enough could stall the process or forfeit the opportunity all together. My best advice— find the proper balances based on your customer and your product and/or service, but make sure your process is efficient.

---

31   Miller, J., (2011). My secret methods for turning marketing leads into qualified sales leads, http://
blog.marketo.com/2011/03/here-are-my-secret-methods-for-turning-marketing-leads-into-qualified-
sales-leads.html

***

Qualification—A Process of Precision Learning

The key to any effective qualification process is precision—a **precise process** that gathers **precise information**, in a **precise way** with **precise timing**. The SAM qualification process is your ability to use precision to load, lock, aim and zero-in on the target information required to close the deal. This information is power and this power shapes your opportunity by identifying the movers, shakers and the ultimate decision-makers. For any sales opportunity the SAM works to understand the 4 Buyer Power Positions:

1. **The Power, Precision and Access to Financial Resources When Ready to Buy**

   a. Does the client have the financial resources to buy?

   b. Are the resources available and accessible?

2. **The Power Precision Authority to Buy**

   a. Does your client have the authority to make the buying decision?

   b. If they do not have the full authority, what level of influence does the client possess and can this influence be used to close the deal?

3. **The Power Precision Need to Buy**

   a. Does the client truly need to buy or is this exploratory?

4. **The Power Precision Timeline to Buy**

   a. Does the client have a timeline to buy and how can you use the timeline to your advantage?

The great challenge and success of understanding client qualification is to appreciate that every business opportunity is not necessarily a "profitable business opportunity." In other words, business opportunities need to have a reasonable assumption that it will result in profitable success. **FACT**—All business is not good business. You must be able to differentiate, segregate, determine, rationalize or factually discover through the qualification process whether this business opportunity is a profitable business opportunity. Remember the time and commitment drain to working non-qualified opportunities will be a drain on your professional success.

Four Key Client Qualification Guidelines

Jonathan Farrington, a globally recognized business coach, mentor, author and consultant, refers to qualification as a vital process and not an event that simply begins and ends one day. Farrington says, *"Only by rigorous questioning will the salesperson be able to answer the following questions when they get back to the office:*

- Is there a requirement / need that my company can satisfy?
- Is it winnable?
- Do I want it?

The very best sales professionals will not pursue the opportunity, after proper objective analysis, if the answer to any of those questions is "No." They would rather invest their precious selling time seeking out and closing opportunities that will provide a profitable return on that investment. At the very highest selling levels: i.e. strategic "big-ticket" selling and marketing, clearly the sales cycle is much more protracted, complex and typically moves through four stages:

1. *Rigorous Opportunity Assessment.*

2. *Develop A Strategy.*

3. *Present The Solution and Re-Assess The Opportunity.*

4. *Gain Formal Commitment, Sign The Order and Develop.*[32]

Farrington's comments make sense to any sales professional and especially the Sales Assassin. We understand the qualification process to be a core competency of the sales profession. This process can be tremendously simple, yet complex when dealing with big-ticket items and sophisticated products and services.

The best fishermen never simply bait a hook, cast and wait for the bite of the big fish. They have scouted the parts of the river where fish lay. They discover the time of day when the fish want to feed and they know the precise bait that drive the fish crazy. When you're prospecting and you've been able to get in front of the decision maker, the same principles apply to the fisherman. One sure way you'll lose that big catch is by not knowing how to introduce your product or service and not asking the right questions so that you can effectively present your bait at the right time and right place—your product or service. Sales 101 teaches us "the greatest salesperson is also the greatest listener." This is true, in part, but as a SAM you know that without having asked the right qualifying questions, the listening is useless. The key to listening is not only hearing the answers to key questions, but also listening to the voice, attitude and body language provided.

---

32   Farrington, Jonathon, 2013. Guest Post: Can you Ask the Tough Questions in the Sales Process?, http://www.thejfblogit.co.uk/tag/opportunity-assessment/#sthash.pVfdJVWW.dpuf

The Art of Asking the Right Questions Without Asking

Master Bruce Lee maintained that his fighting style was the *Art of Fighting without Fighting*, meaning having the ability to win without actually having to fight. Likewise, in client qualification, I call this process the *Art of Asking Questions without Asking*.

A SAM must learn to extract as much information as possible and be able to capture it in a very short period of time. That information you extract must allow you to assess what your customer's needs are—then you must find a way to do it without them even realizing it. I truly consider it an art form because you have to use "finesse without offense" within the first two minutes of your introduction" to get them off the defense in the very beginning of the call. Finesse might sound like an inappropriate word to use but consider the alternative. If they sense that you're a bloodsucker only interested in closing them, game over. This is essential! It's all about building a rapport and then "staging" a conversation with your potential client in such a way that they're giving you the info you need for your closing arsenal. By doing so, you're getting him or her involved in the sales process and making them feel like they're playing an important role. A SAM is able to ascertain if there's even an opportunity to do business within the first 2 minutes of the call.

Technical qualifying using "Hot Spots"

Qualifying is an unbelievably important part of the sales process, especially in today's age of hyper technology and having instant access to information via your smartphone. Consumers have become well informed and incredibly intelligent about everything. But here's the key: you have to be more knowledgeable and better equipped to assess their needs than they are, otherwise, what do they need you for? Earlier in this book we've discussed the importance of having intimate knowledge of your product or service. The qualification process is when you'll put this skill to use because this is when you'll focus on key "hot spots" with your potential buyer in order to make the sale. For example, are they looking for better quality? Are they looking for a better price? Is service what's the most important to them? Is it a combo of all three or is it something else entirely? Being able to isolate the hot spots in order to assess need requires a mastery level of technical qualifying skills, especially when your prospect is "cold" and doesn't realize the need exists.

As I mentioned earlier, my primary business is in manufacturing and global distribution of hard Italian cheeses. I'm known in the industry as The Big Cheese AKA The Cheese Boss. You'd be amazed to know that over 4.2 billion pounds of Italian cheeses are produced in the US each year and the type of cheese I sell is grated, shredded and shaved hard Italian cheeses (i.e. Parmesan, Romano, Asiago and blends). One of my pitches is "we custom blend based on price and quality." Custom blend? Yes, that's right, custom blend. If I told you how intricate the grated cheese business is and how incredibly important the qualification process is to get to the finish line, you'd be amazed. For example, when I'm speaking to a potential buyer I need to know key pieces of information: i.e. is this for a new project or an existing project; is there a specification sheet available for review; can we obtain a sample for analysis and flavor profiling, what is the product application, estimated usage, distribution; what quality is required (high grade, medium grade or low grade); what price point do I need to meet, etc. And if I cannot extract this data during my first conversation or first couple of emails then I've most likely decreased my chances of closing the sale. This is an example of knowing my product and knowing the right technical qualifying questions to ask so that I can isolate the hot spots and close the sale.

The Cheese Boss and The Cake Boss!

If you are new to a company or new to the business you're in, then it takes time to learn your product and to know exactly what info you need to extract in order to gain new business. However, as a SAM, when you know your products inside and out you'll quickly learn what the "hot spots" are and what the majority of your client base is looking for. The quicker you isolate those "hot spots," the quicker you'll be able to determine if you have a viable opportunity to sell or not.

Four Parts to Qualification Questioning:

Part 1: Pre-meeting Research

Your pre-meeting research will be the basis of meeting success. Use their website as a key source of information. Remember that their Facebook page and Twitter feeds will also provide current updates. Use LinkedIn as a primary source of information for the key players. Key research items include:

- Knowledge of the client's business:
  - ➤ Demographics and scope of business, products and services offered
  - ➤ Who are the key players and know their background, especially know the background of people with whom you will be meeting
  - ➤ Understand current business issues
  - ➤ Competitor information

Part 2: Pre-meeting Preparation and Organization

After completing your research, organize the information obtained in a logical sequence for you to use it. Develop your qualifying questions and anticipate hot spots—those crucial issues that are very important to the client. It is important to understand the questioning process has several objectives:

- To gain answers and further insights beyond your research for information you do not know or understand or have access to

- Even though you may already know certain information, great questions can serve to demonstrate your interest and desire to learn more

Part 3: Meeting Execution

Learning to control a sales meeting can be a tricky proposition. The following advice will guide you to success:

- Learn to take quick notes. Trying to capture every word is a recipe for failure and can keep you from making that all-important eye contact. Even if you are doing a conference call, you must try to capture the essence of the spirit of the conversation

- Use targeted questions to control the meeting

- Avoid the tendency to attack the client with your sales pitch

- Immediately express appreciation for the opportunity to learn about the company. Your appreciation is not a thanks for allowing you to talk about you and your product. Remember, this is an opportunity to learn and share—selling is the result of learning and sharing and solving problems

- Tap into the client's emotions, frustrations, needs, expectations and concerns.

- Seek to discover the client's decision-making process and hierarchy

- Seek to understand their expectations of vendors

- Leave the meeting with an agreed list of action items

Part 4: Post-Meeting Data Gathering and Next Step Preparation

Back in your office, it's time to pull all this valuable information together in a form to allow you to plan your next steps for action items. Expand your notes from the short-hand notes taken during the meeting. Failure to do this quickly will result in not being able to recall some of the important details of the meeting. The following is a list of post-meeting data assimilation and next step preparation:

- Do not overwhelm your client with information immediately after the meeting. Thank them for their time, the opportunity to learn about the organization and provide them the information they ask for—no more and no less

- Follow-up in a timely fashion—2 to 3 days is best

- Differentiate your follow-up from others. Most of us think email is the only way in this era to converse. Hard-copy mail still works and can make you stand out from others

- Make your follow-up short, professional and to the point. Avoid the temptation to try to close the deal too quickly

The ability to recognize the potential and then "lead" and convert that customer.

The Client Qualification Process Matters

Perfecting your client qualification skills is an art form for a SAM. Like any skill, this skill is learned and mastered through constant training and conditioning. You have to practice, practice and practice some more. Create a client qualification work sheet that contains all of the essential information you need to gather from your buyer. Put your qualifying skills into practice, learn how and what you need to say just as much as what you need to AVOID saying. Hone in on what's working by evaluating each conversation. Study your qualification questions line by line and ask yourself these questions:

1. Did my customer respond well to this particular question?
2. Did I offend my customer when I asked him that particular question?
3. Were there any irrelevant questions?
4. Did my customer understand my product and was I able to gather information based on my presentation?
5. Did I isolate the "hot spots" or was I afraid to ask?
6. When I got back to my office and read my notes, what did I discover? Did I have all the necessary information? Could I put together a clear profile and story about this client? What were the gaps in the story? What other information do I need to obtain?

Once you've been able to master the client qualification process that applies to your sector of sales, whether it's cars, insurance, gadgets, food, B2C or B2B, I guarantee you that you'll see a positive difference in your closing ratio and overall sales success. Proper qualification is the difference between closing the sale and not getting the business! Remember, whatever you sell, no matter what it is and to whom you're selling, there's competition. The person who qualifies the best wins and is on the direct path to becoming a SAM!

5 Techniques to Qualification Mastery

1. *Search and Discover the Emotional Drivers of Your Client*

Emotions are integral to almost everything we do. It may be the off-hand comments that are clues to client thinking and motivation. It is these emotional clues that may lead to understanding what may be driving or may actually drive the final decision to not only buy, but who may be the person that I will buy from. Tune in to how you may offer relief or a solution to these drivers. When appropriate, relate to the issue with examples of other clients or your own experiences that better connect you to the clients and their needs. This emotional connect can lead to loyalty and future opportunity even if this sales opportunity does not come together.

2. Focus On Your Client's Needs

In most cases clients come to us with thoughts, ideas, concepts and preconceived ideas of what they think they need. However, these preconceived ideas may be misguided and can evolve if you know how to create a client self-discovery of needs process. In fact, your questions, when properly formatted, will often make them rethink their preconceived notions. Honing in on client needs is the result of asking questions, listening to responses and re-questioning new ideas and concepts, working to solutions and eventually excitement. If there are missing facts or something is unclear, it is important to ask the client simple and concise questions: gathering data will become a much easier process and in the meantime, you will avoid creating a sense of misunderstanding with the client. The goal: what does my client need? Not what I want them to need and what I want to sell them.

One of the best examples of this point is a trip to your local big-box electronic store in search for a new computer. Too often these sales professionals are on a mission—commission by selling me a bigger, faster and fancier piece of equipment than what I need. What I want is a computer and software that is simple to use and helps me organize my day-to-day life in a more simple manner. My needs in this case are very different than a small business that needs a computer and software to help manage business inventory and finances. The question you must ask yourself is—**What information do I have to gather from the client to be sure I present them a solution?**

You may be tempted to sell your client your top-of-the-line computer and software, when they really only need the baseline model. By over-selling them more than they need, you may jeopardize future business opportunity. Customers are savvy and will eventually figure out that they don't need most of what you sold them. Now you have a bitter and resentful customer who sees you having wasted their money and not looking out for their best interest. They'll see you as a "salesperson" and not as a resource.

3. *Personalize Your Language to Your Client*

Your client is a person, not a thing. The way you speak can be a clear message to the client of what you think about them. The word "YOU" can be powerful. Overuse of the word "I" can be a turnoff. Letting the client know that your every thought revolves around them gives indication of a personal connection and your desire to serve them and solve their problems. Changing the way you speak and the terms you use makes a difference in how you are received by your client. Using "you," "yours," or "you will find," "you will discover" rather than "I think," "I believe," "I know" or "Let me tell you about," directs your message to a much more personal level.

4. *Help Your Client See Financial Value and the Return on Investment*

Just like you, your client is trying to make money. If you know your product can help your client save money and increase profitability, then make sure they understand the specific return on investment in terms of dollars and cents. If your product has features that differentiate you from the competition then you may have a valuable advantage.

5. *Discover and Leverage Your Client's Priorities*

When businesses look to improve their operations, they call on sales professionals and consultants for new products and services. However, these professionals can do very little to help their clients if they cannot identify and understand the client's priorities and how these priorities relate to their business objectives. Knowing the client's priorities then leads to understanding the client's alternatives. These alternatives allow the client options to meet their goals and objectives under different constraints and circumstances that are present today or may evolve. To figure out priorities and constraint alternatives, consultants have to gather and analyze as much data about the company and the industry as possible. A SAM training imperative is possessing a relentless knowledge of the importance of your product and its benefits to your client. If you've listened to the client and determined their needs, but still are not progressing in closing the deal, find out if there are other elements of their business that are taking priority and pushing your sale aside. Simply, if you know your client is pushing through the implementation of a high priority project that takes precedence over your product sale, acknowledge your appreciation and understanding of this priority and work to position your follow up for a later date that coincides with client needs. Schedule a callback at a later date that may stand a better chance of getting some attention. To do this you have to ask the questions because the information is not always volunteered. Again, focus on the needs, expectations, demands and priorities of your client. Make this effort the foundation of a longer term relationship—the issue is not "now or never" but rather "not now is not never but focused on forever."

Watch Out—The No Power (No-Po) Beasts, AKA "Non-Decision-makers" Are Lurking Around Every Corner

There are 3 words that can drive a salesperson crazy—maybe, perhaps, possibly. When these words are even hinted at, we get into gear and begin to jump, beg, borrow, steal, spin, chase, and beg. The hunt is on and the cycle of chasing the wrong people begins. Who are these unknown decision-makers wielding so much power? Who are these obstacles whose sheer existence drives sales professionals into chasing their tail in madness. Before exploring the intricacies of client qualification a sales professional must first understand how to deal with some of the most powerful players in any sales scenario.

***

The No-Po's

These "Guardians of the Salesgate" are a mysterious breed that can destroy all hope, or may simply use their keys to unlock the door to success.

***

No-Po's Job Description

The No-Power Beast, aka "No-Po" is someone whose unwitting role is to generate a sense of false hope and security in the sales professional. They can be low in the hierarchical chain of a company but are mammoth in their consumption of energy in any attempt to close the deal. The No-Po is also a being of mystical corporate power that we bow and pay homage to for their ability to hypnotize us, eliciting a sense of false hope and progress. In simple terms the No-Po is a person who in reality has no real decision making power in any sales scenario. However, the role they play can thwart your best sales efforts. These individuals are generally the first line of contact in the client's office. It could be the receptionist, office manager or any individual who is the first line of defense—"The Gatekeeper."

The No-Po Challenge

Reflect on the following points to determine your propensity to be captive in the spell of No-Po influence. *Is this you?*

1. I am impressed with the intellectual capacity of my No-Po's. They speak a language that gives me hope and a sense of security when I leave their office.

2. I want to believe that all things good are on the brink of happening if I can just take one more step. Therefore, I am patient and listen with all interest for those kernels of hope.

3. Now that I have my No-Po in the palm of my hand, all I have to do is get an audience with their boss. I've given them my best stuff and I'm sure they are impressed with me. I've done a great job convincing them, and now it's time to convince their boss—now it's time to fret, ponder and wonder when will the boss walk in.

4. My last meeting was fabulous. Today is the day. Here they come—I think? Or is this more of the "maybe or perhaps" team. In any case I think I am making more progress.

5. I've been introduced to more people—most of them are from the "maybe" school, but I believe I am getting closer.

6. Finally, I've paid my dues. It's time for No-Po's to deliver. They have to feel guilty for the all the time I've spent cultivating this relationship.

As you have gone through each of these scenarios, how do you feel? Are you too embarrassed to acknowledge except in the deep reaches of your mind that you are one of those who gets sucked into the No-Po Trance?

Your greatest concern must be not to fall victim to the disease called "The Sales Scotoma Block." A scotoma is a mental blind-spot that inhibits us from seeing the reality of life. The SSB disease can be treated, but it takes discipline and confidence. As a SAM, the will to fight the SSB must become a natural part of everyday sales life.

The antidote to the No-Po dilemma is simple but takes commitment. Reflect on the following points to determine your propensity to be captive in the spell of the No-Po influence. *Is this you?*

1. Clearly identify the key influencer and/or decision-maker and his or her relationship to the No-Po.

2. Determine if the No-Po truly has access to the decision-maker. If not, seek a new path and new relationships.

3. If new relationships are not available, you must determine the barriers—the break-through action that will change the

nature of the engagement. This is a big challenge. Remember, the root issue may not be the No-Po. It may be you and your inability to differentiate yourself from the competition.

4. Change the paradigm—Make sure you are using SAM Power. The search for SAM Power is your ability to powerfully influence and change the dynamics of the relationship.

   a. Discover the power words that will influence this client. Explore what is important to them, not what you think is important.

   b. Do more client research on the most recent issues impacting the company's success.

   c. Strategic and impactful use and leverage of your new knowledge and high impact power words.

   d. Isolate conversation to focus on high impact solutions to the client's needs, always referring back to the client's clearly defined issues. Repeat and reconfirm the issues.

Now Close the No-Po Gap

➤ **You've Got the No-Po's Attention:** How? You've identified the key issues and needs.

➤ **You've Got a Dynamic Solution:** You have solved the problem the client presented you.

➤ **You've Differentiated Yourself:** You have clearly stated why you are different from the competition and what you can do for the client that competitors can not.

➤ **You've Positioned Yourself:** You have positioned yourself as a valuable resource and ally for present and future business solutions.

> ➤ **You've Established a Level of Integrity:** A partnership
> has begun based upon a respectful and trusted relationship
> between you and the client.

No-Po Example at Work

*Like most people I've had a long-term relationship with my general
practitioner doctor. Most of us spend a good amount of time waiting
to be called in from the waiting room. I've come to know the office
manager and receptionist quite well. Whether you're sitting in the
Doc's office or the dentist's office you will often notice polished young
professionals sitting in the waiting room along with patients. You
can spot these well dressed individuals toting fully loaded bags with
the latest in pharmaceutical samples they are hoping to market to
the doctor. The sales professionals are far from achieving SAM status
as they are still held at arms length by the guardians at the gate—
No Po's, aka Office Managers. The famous words uttered by these
guardians are simply, "I'm sorry but Doctor Welby is behind in his
appointments and may not be able to see you today. Please feel free to
leave me some literature and samples and I'll be sure he gets them."
The Pharma Sales Rep yields to the power of the gate-keeper and
heads to the next office down the hall. I can now read their mind, "I
hope Dr. Welby gets the information and samples. I'll follow up next
week."*

Defeat?

The central question is what would a SAM do in the same
scenario? The answer is clear. The SAM would have preceded
his or her visits with a series of strategically placed phone calls,
email communications and online research, all designed to build
a relationship with key staff decision makers and the No-Po. The
key would be to establish yourself, your name and your product

before sitting listlessly in the waiting rooms for countless hours hoping for your star-struck encounter with Dr. Welby. Again, the qualification process takes work and the ability to manage diverse and at times difficult relationships. This work will pay off if it is done in a strategic and tactical way.

Lessons from the Ultimate Sales Assassin on Client Qualification

1. The key to any effective qualification process is precision—a **precise process** that gathers **precise information**, in a **precise way** with **precise timing**.

2. The No-Po's—The "Guardians of the Sales gate" are a formidable obstacle that can destroy all hope or may simply use their keys to unlock the door to success.

3. Like any skill, the client qualification skill is learned and mastered thru constant practice and conditioning. You have to practice, practice and practice some more.

4. Gathering precise information in a precise way with precise timing means nothing if you never ask for the sale!

CHAPTER 7

SAM BELT 6:
THE MASTERY OF LEADERSHIP
INTEGRITY

"First, you tell the truth to yourself about yourself. Then you tell the truth to yourself about another. At the third level, you tell the truth about yourself to another. Then you tell your truth about another to that other. And finally, you tell the truth to everyone about everything."[33]
—Neale Donald Walsch

YOU CANNOT BE the "Master" of anything unless you are a Master of Leadership. Your leadership strength must become a reality, and your reality in mastery of any discipline is to be a model of leadership in every aspect of the work we do. Long ago I came to understand leadership has little to do with hierarchical titles and who reports to whom. Instead, leadership is the behavior we exhibit to the world around us. Leadership becomes the example we set in how we get things done each day, how we embrace challenges. How we demonstrate performance excellence. Leadership is how a SAM differentiates his or herself from the competition. Leadership defines our code of conduct in that every success is the result of mastery of truthfulness and integrity, traits that far too many sales

---

33 King, Gary. The Power of Truth, http://www.thepoweroftruth.com/truth_quotes.html

professionals have yet to embrace. Each and every sales professional must be a leader—a person who is willing to take control over the sales environment and every sales engagement and lead customers to a close by being trustworthy, truthful and possessing integrity as a core of who you are.

Do you know what it means to be a trustworthy, truthful and high integrity person? I've thought a lot about this over the years and I challenge myself on these characteristics each day. These issues come into play in every sales engagement I have. Why is it that so many sales professionals fail to understand that how they function, make decisions and communicate their decisions demonstrates to their customers whether they can be trusted? For example, it is like the way we approach ethics. For many it is about how to avoid embarrassment and illegality, rather than how to create strength and trust. It is a denial of ultimate responsibility. Only when we take that responsibility do we create the trust that matters. Integrity is what we achieve when we live each day with honesty and respect for our customers and with a clear sense of our values and purpose in our lives and the work we do.

How can you determine if you are a good leader, or even a great leader possessing the highest levels of integrity? What are your strengths and what are your weaknesses? I prefer to call them *improvement opportunities*. I am not perfect, but do any of my imperfections rise to the level of derailing my business or my career?

We can see and feel integrity in people. We see self-confidence and strength of conviction and a willingness to stand for those things that are right. Integrity does not know arrogance and possesses a proper balance of humility and is committed to success, yet not willing to run over others for personal gain. When our integrity flourishes, we know our limits and stay in context of what is right, fighting off urges to cut corners. Those with integrity are not manipulated by others and do not follow the crowd. As a SAM, I must possess a high level of self-confidence that I can and will achieve success. However, through my successes and especially through my failures I've learned humility. It is this humility that balances and grounds me today. This humility is what differentiates the SAM from the sales professional who is arrogant and demonstrates an exaggerated sense of their own importance and abilities.

In tough business dynamics, it is the "NO" decisions that determine our trustworthiness and integrity. When we are willing to sacrifice our own gratification to maintain our values, then we are becoming a person of integrity and a true leader within the SAM environment. Customers can spot salespeople who lack integrity and become leery of the sales professional because they judge all salespeople the same and as untrustworthy. Listen, I was both a stock broker and a mortgage broker and I know how I was perceived. I had everything to do with creating that perception. When I dealt with my clients, I was silver-tongued, quick-witted and clever. When I trained rookie stock brokers I was hardcore. I used those cliché mantras like ABC "Always Be Closing" and even created some new ones of my own like "Sell Ice to Eskimos." I thought they wrote movies like Wall Street and Boiler Room about me. I admit it; I loved being a young salesperson and I loved, above all else, that I was outrageously persuasive and influential. I lived the lifestyle and it quenched my thirst. However, when circumstances occur, lessons are learned, and that well runs dry, a SAM learns that in business, humility and integrity trumps self-gratification and conspicuous consumption every time.

For me, especially as a SAM, integrity has become the most sacred and important of all my values. I've learned that my reputation in business is what sustains me both professionally and personally. To preserve and strengthen my integrity demands that I cannot live or work for the approval of others, and that I must know what professionalism and success really means.

Seldom does much time go by when I don't ask myself or ask my business manager, Krystal, how am I doing in running my business? Asking her that question I had better be sitting down and ready for the answer because she will tell me like it is. The great part of our relationship over the years has been the honesty that goes between us. Being honest with myself, the real questions I'm asking are:

- How am I leading this sales business?
- Am I leading by example?
- Do I practice what I preach?
- Am I leading with integrity? Does my team trust me and respect me? Do I demonstrate and show trust in them?

Successful SAM leadership requires you not only lead with integrity, but be willing to receive feedback no matter how painful that feedback may be. The irony is we generally know when we are being a good leader, but the validation by others is our reality check.

Your leadership integrity begins with a self-assessment challenge. Rate yourself against the following 10 questions. After rating yourself, ask a colleague, friend and maybe better yet, ask your spouse to rate you.

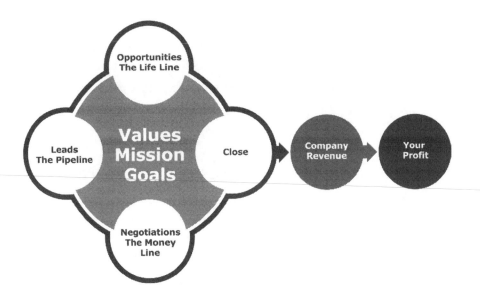

Maximizing Values, Mission and Goals

SAM Leadership Integrity Self-Assessment

1. I maintain a positive attitude in the most difficult circumstances.

   Strongly Agree   Agree   Don't Agree

2. I can calm myself when under great stress.

   Strongly Agree   Agree   Don't Agree

3. When things go wrong I accept responsibility.

   Strongly Agree   Agree   Don't Agree

4. I never stretch the truth to customers about my products and services.

   Strongly Agree   Agree   Don't Agree

5. I have a reputation for being honest with my clients.

   Strongly Agree   Agree   Don't Agree

6. My team, my teammates and my supervisor think that I am trustworthy.

   Strongly Agree   Agree   Don't Agree

7. I am a role model to people I work with and those with whom I do business.

   Strongly Agree   Agree   Don't Agree

8. My colleagues come to me with problems because I seek a win/win solution.

   Strongly Agree   Agree   Don't Agree

9. I am approachable and humble.

   Strongly Agree   Agree   Don't Agree

10. I accept responsibility for my mistakes in business and life.

   Strongly Agree   Agree   Don't Agree

If you are like most people, this self-assessment highlights things that you MUST work on to get better. This is another part of the self-discovery and self-development concept that I want to reinforce. Remember, improvement is always a work in progress.

As a martial artist, you learn that your power comes from your core. Not just the core of your body, but the core of your mind and heart. The most powerful front-kick comes from harnessing these tools and allowing them to work together as an explosive weapon. So too is leadership. It comes from your core and it is also the place where your leadership ethics reside. It is from your core where you will find your power to persevere.

The Sales Assassin Master must learn **3 Power-Kick Leadership Principles.** These principles come from your core:

1. <u>**Grounded In Sales Ethics, Truthfulness and Integrity**</u>

    Truthfulness and Integrity must be at the core of your moral fiber. Trust is the reward we receive when people realize our level of integrity. Ethics are the foundation on which our integrity and trust are built.

    - Truthfulness and Integrity mean being personally and professionally responsible and accountable

    - Providing the truth with professionalism

    - Acknowledging your shortcomings

    - Providing an honest representation of products and services you provide

    - Never misrepresenting yourself or your products and services for your personal gain

2. <u>Recognize When Your Integrity Is Being Tested</u>

Once you lose your integrity, regaining it is nearly impossible. As a sales broker in many different industries, sometimes it took having the instinct and a conscience to know when to disengage from an opportunity. A SAM quickly realizes that long-term integrity, safety and well-being far outweigh short-term gain. You must recognize when your integrity is being tested; and it will be tested each day. Here is an "outrageous" question: Is your integrity for sale? It better not be or else your SAM goal is dead before it starts. Integrity is a personal choice. In your most driven state of mind for the sale, a SAM cannot compromise his or her future success. To a SAM, your values and your integrity are worth more than this week's paycheck. You cannot put your integrity up for sale to the highest bidder. If you do, you had better understand that you can't buy it back. All you have is your integrity. It must be a prized possession. These days integrity is not a commodity. It is often a rare trait of professionals in many industries. As a SAM, you must have personal dignity. Each of us is proud of our accomplishments in both our professional and personal lives. These lead us to being willing, able and eager to accept new challenges. However, these challenges will present to us situations that will test our character and may compromise our dignity. We must accept that the ability to maintain our dignity is all about self-respect, the confidence and pride we possess and our ability to do business in a fair and professional way. This is dignity and with it you will achieve integrity.

The true SAM leader understands that a lack of integrity may result in a short-term gain or a quick sale or profit, but it will also result in a loss of long-term success, relationships and a sustainable business. Once you lose your integrity, regaining it is nearly impossible.

3. <u>**Values and Beliefs Define Your SAM Passion, Dedication and Courage**</u>

If you remember, we said in Belt 1 that SAM Passion, Dedication and Courage require an outrageous commitment to persevere your greatest obstacles. We defined PDC as the holy trinity of the sales professional's heart, mind and spirit. We said it will drive success in the best and worst of times. Now we must go a step further and accept that outrageous PDC cannot offend our personal values, sensibilities and beliefs.

Whether you consciously or unconsciously act on desires and passions that don't resonate with your core values and beliefs, it eventually results in a disruptive internal conflict. When you have this confusion inside, you will never experience true happiness or satisfaction. This disruption is a thief that robs you of your sense of peace with yourself, happiness, and can leave you feeling frustrated. We have all desired something in life, and used that desire to excuse behavior that conflicts with our deep down sense of right and wrong. When this happens it's easy to minimize the situation by telling ourselves that it's just a little thing that doesn't really matter. Even when you don't realize it, there is still a price to pay for not following your internal moral compass.

The challenge is that in our core we create a war within ourselves. As I said earlier, if your mindset is not in the right framework, you do not allow yourself to self-correct. Sooner or later your internal conflict will destroy your success and undermine what you have worked so hard to achieve.

As a SAM, you must accept that leadership is all about your behavior and the integrity that guides your leadership each day. Integrity is the core of leadership and the most vital of all characteristics. It lives and breathes by your ability to be consistent in your actions, the ways you think and behave, the expectations you set for yourself and others and outcomes you achieve. The world of SAM leaders excels at our commitment to do things the right way.

Our relationships are built on a solid platform of trust and seek never to break the sacred trust of customers and others who place their faith in us. Avoid arrogance, fretting and fearing things you cannot control, negativity and buying into short cuts..

> *"Great Leadership is a product of great integrity."*[34]
> —Abraham Lincoln

The greatest lessons in leadership integrity, I have learned, comes from failures and frailties of others who have been a part of my life. I learned that I must treat people with respect and dignity. I remember the pain and agony of working for and with people who lack the ability to lead without selfishness. I challenge all leaders to live and lead with integrity. You will not only benefit the people you lead, but also enjoy more personal and professional satisfaction.

---

34   Hopkins, Michael R., 2012. Leadership and Integrity, http://leadonpurposeblog.com/2012/01/21/leadership-and-integrity/

10 Irrefutable Challenges of SAM Sales Leadership

1. **Successful SAM leaders live behaviors that demonstrate integrity in all they do.**

   - The SAM will always learn from both success and failure in life. In these successes and failures, the SAM will treat others with respect and dignity.

2. **Successful SAM leaders continue to improve their knowledge of their product market and seek to change and refocus when necessary.**

   - SAM leadership requires an in-depth understanding of the marketplace where they work. They will also embrace the reality of marketplace dynamics, adapting sales strategy to new demands and expectations.

3. **Successful SAM leaders practice relentless communication at all levels of the business.**

   - Relentless communication has no end point whether directed at customers, senior management or suppliers: a SAM will realize strength and better positioning for success when effectively communicating situations, circumstance and progress against goals and sales opportunities.

4. **Successful SAM leaders demonstrate Passion, Dedication and Courage.**

   - Remember, a Sales Assassin Master will never be denied, for you have achieved Passion, Dedication and Courage. As a leader, your business sword will be sharp and precise. You will move with precision and confidence through your sales journey. You will be strong as a leader and dedicated to growing personally and professionally. You will have a passion and commitment to yourself, your company and products. You will be loyal to customers but maintain a balanced approach to the business, using integrity as your guide.

5. **Successful SAM leaders continuously, relentlessly and with integrity communicate the value of their products and services.**

    • Relentless communication establishes and sustains relationships with customers. Your communication is a contagious characteristic that will serve all those around you.

6. **Successful SAM leaders not only communicate well, they learn the art of dynamic presentation.**

    • The practice of relentless communications is a skill that you must embrace, but dynamic presentation is an art that must be practiced and then mastered. The voice you use, your body language, the way you sit all provide a message and establish your presence as leader—a person who is confident in himself and a master of their expertise.

7. **Successful SAM leaders are willing to make difficult decisions and willing to take prudent, high-integrity risks each day.**

    • SAM leaders know when, why and how to cut their losses.

8. **Successful SAM leaders are results-driven and growth-oriented.**

    • Achieving results and growth in any business is based on commitment. Commitment from your core.

Remember, your core is your body, mind and spirit. A SAM is a builder, refiner and executor of a sales strategy based on your ability to learn from past experience, knowledge of the market, and best practices.

9. **Successful SAM leaders are willing to confront their greatest fears.**

- What are your greatest fears as a sales leader? The great sales professional and consultant **Brian Tracy** describes fear in this way:

  "The most successful sales people work continually to confront the fears that hold most sales people back. The two major fears that stand as the greatest obstacles on your road to success are the fear of failure, and the fear of criticism or rejection.

  As it happens, it's the fear of failure or rejection that holds you back. It is the anticipation of fear or rejection that paralyzes you and holds you back from doing what you need to do in the first place.

  You have to remember that everyone is afraid. The difference between the hero and the coward is that the hero is brave just a couple of minutes longer. Everyone you meet is afraid of failure and rejection. But the brave person confronts the fear and does it anyway. The average person on the other hand, moves away from the fear and avoids the fear-causing situation.

  Here are the most powerful words you can use to overcome your fears of failure and rejection. Just say to yourself over and over again whenever you start to become nervous or anxious about anything: "I can do it, I can do it, I can do it."

  And here's the good news. The more you repeat the words, "I can do it," the lower are your fears and the higher is your *self-esteem and self-confidence. As you say the words, "I like myself. I'm the best of the best. I can do it," you raise your self-esteem and self-confidence to the point where you feel unstoppable. This is the mindset you want to have to learn <u>how to sell</u> more." [35]*

10. Successful SAM leaders have a vision for success and possess contagious optimism for this success.

- None of us has a crystal ball that will forecast the future. However, as a leader, I have a vision of my success and belief in that vision; my belief that I can achieve greatness will never be relinquished.

Urijah Faber, former WEC/UFC Champion, ranked the #3 MMA bantamweight in the world describes his insane brand of confidence and optimism in his book The Laws of The Ring:

"At some point between my first and second professional fights, when the prospect of making a career in a sport that then consisted of competing in semi-illegal fights on Indian reservations was still a wild long shot, I sat around with a group of friends and talked about my big plans. I have a tendency to do this—I just can't help it. I'm a motivational guy, and I want everyone around me to feel the same way.

During this particular conversation, my buddy Will Creger interrupted me and asked, "Why are you so confident about EVERYTHING? Where does that come from?" His tone wasn't angry or challenging. My attitude just blew him away, and he was both curious and amused.

It's just the way I am. I make a point to stay positive and I'm always looking forward to the next thing to feed my

---

35   Tracy, Brian. http://www.briantracy.com/blog/sales-success/
best-of-the-best-how-to-sell-like-most-successful/attachment/most-successful-salespeople/

excitement. When something bad happens in my life, I'm pretty good at shrugging it off and going forward. In reality you have to anyway, right?"[36]

Lessons From the Ultimate Sales Assassin Master:

1. Remember your personal values, the things that make you unique and those things that people have admired about who you are.
2. Integrate your values into your SAM Leadership Mentality.
3. Never compromise for a quick buck or win.
4. Practice what you preach: Live and breathe your SAM Leadership Integrity.

---

36   http://www.amazon.com/Laws-Ring-Urijah-Faber/dp/B00B9ZF0HI

Sales Assassin Developmental Assessment

Recognizing the Sales Leadership Influences in Your Life

1. In the earliest portions of your professional life, who are the leaders who had the greatest influence on who you are today?

   a. Which of these leaders demonstrated the leadership behavior as we have defined a SAM leader?

   b. What were the behaviors that you respected in them?

   c. How did they demonstrate being ethically grounded?

   d. What specifically did you see and learn from these individuals?

   Positive and negative?

2. We see leaders in public view everyday on television and on the Internet. Identify public leaders you admire and those you do not admire. Why? Remember, the question is about how they lead, not whether you agree with their politics.

   a. Who do you admire? Why?

   b. Who don't you admire? Why?

   c. What did you learn from each?

CHAPTER 8

SAM BELT 7: REINVESTMENT IN YOUR BUSINESS AND YOU

"Engage people with what they expect; it is what they are able to discern and confirms their projections. It settles them into predictable patterns of response, occupying their minds while you wait for the extraordinary moment—that which they cannot anticipate."[37]

—Sun Tzu, The Art of War

Self-Discovery of the YOU in Sales Assassin Mastery

You and your business cannot sustain success and profitability without reinvesting, reinforcing and or nourishing the foundation of success. You and your business need strength—continual preparation and conditioning of all the elements of your business. Strength comes by the building of muscle and reinforcing the bones of your business—continuing to build your SAM DNA. The concept is easy to understand. YOU are your business; your business is YOU. As I noted in the introduction to this book, no matter if you work for a company or whether you're a business owner, a salesperson must treat the profession as being in business

---

37   Sun Tzu. On the Art of War, Translation by Lionel Giles, http://www.artofwarsuntzu.com/Art%20of%20War%20PDF.pdf

for themselves. Read it again. *You must treat the sales profession as being in business for yourself.* What does this mean? A SAM must be an entrepreneur no matter what name is on your title. Quite simply, only investing time and resources into mastering product or service knowledge is not sufficient enough to guarantee your sales success. If you're the owner/operator of "ACME Widgets," no question that you must invest in knowing all of the intricate details of "ACME Widgets," their functionality, their multi-uses, variations, benefits, price points, upgrades, and the whole nine yards. However, you better realize that your business strength and the one thing that will turn "widgets" into "profits" is YOU. Yes, knowledge is everything but YOU are more. Without your personal growth the chance of you achieving all of your sales targets and goals is highly unlikely. Reinvesting into the business of "You" means investing time and resources into learning about how to be a better salesperson and a better you.

It Takes Money to Make Money... Invest!

In the introduction I assumed the fact that you are reading this book is proof that you've already accepted the concept that you must invest in your business. Buying this book, attending sales seminars, watching videos and listening to tapes is all a part of the hundreds of dollars sales professionals invest to make a difference in their career. Remember, you must be honest with yourself. What has been your ROI? I'm willing to bet you're still trying to cash in on your investments. To achieve SAM status you must be willing to make a bigger investment and accept a certain amount of risk.

If you own "ACME Widgets, Inc." you probably have some technical certification that certifies your knowledge of the design and development of this product. This is an investment. You had to develop a business plan describing your organization, market research, your product line and secondary services, your marketing strategy, financial projections, and funding. This is an investment. You need office space or other brick and mortar, equipment, maybe inventory and warehousing, operational structure, perhaps support personnel, etc. These are all investments. And while making these investments does contribute to what would appear to be a sound and solid foundation, "ACME Widgets, Inc." might not see its second year in business UNLESS you, the owner, reinvests in learning and polishing the skill sets required to make, market and SELL your widgets to your customer base! A SAM will constantly reinvest in his or her business and knows that his or her customers aren't just buying the product; they are also buying YOU—the world's leading expert on ACME Widgets and how they will solve a problem or meet a need.

Invest in Creating the Competitive Distinction...Create a New Value Proposition

Never be surprised when the competition raises its ugly head, ready to take control of what you have worked so hard to achieve. When "ABCD Widgets, Inc." opens selling similar widgets to ACME brand widgets, you better assume and prepare that ABCD also has a solid operation. What does your business do? How do YOU react and respond to competition? A SAM will accelerate into high gear and go on a mission to figure out how to maintain or gain the advantage over your new competitor. It's time to differentiate yourself and create a positive distinction and *recognition* from your competition!

"The best revenge is massive success."[38]
—Frank Sinatra

***

Creating a positive, unique message is a marketing strategy that businesses use to differentiate themselves from the competition. This is the concept developing your personal brand—the traits that differentiate YOU from your competition. Your differentiation strategy must target a segment of the market and deliver a clear and distinct message that the product and what you are offering is clearly different and superior to anything else the customer can possibly experience.

Create a new value proposition for your business that defines clearly a different strategy to focus on the value of your product compared to other similar products from your competitors. When savvy consumers see and feel that you offer a unique product and are a trusted resource, they will want YOU as a partner. Your value proposition creates a new recognition, it may highlight cost saving, sustainability and durability of you and your product compared to your competitor.

The SAM value proposition also allows you to compete beyond the traditional price warfare that the typical sales pro will try to deliver. For example, car companies are experts in this arena, but the car salesman can blow the differentiation by assuming it's all about the dollars. Car manufacturers go to great extremes to differentiate their products and make the customer feel that their cars are desirable and that you will acquire that desirability if you buy their car. This differentiation can entice the customer to spend

---

38   The Inspiration Engine, http://theinspirationengine.blogspot.com/2012/02/best-revenge-is-massive-success.html

more than originally planned. The SAM car salespro feels they have clearly differentiated their line of cars as an image enhancer or status symbol, while other car companies focus only on cost savings.

A SAM realizes that the goal is to create the very real feeling that there is no substitute for you and the brand you represent. Consumers can be very brand loyal especially when it is perceived that what you offer is quality. The SAM continues to deliver quality or value to consumers to maintain the earned loyalty. This loyalty can become a differentiation in and of itself. Loyalty is a selling point and market differentiator.

Case Study of Loyalty: The Product Differentiator

MaryAnn Falkenberg has been a real estate sales professional for over 50 years. At age 82, she remains a top agent in the highly competitive Northwest Chicago real estate market. *"I began like many real estate agents struggling to get listings and selling houses 7 days a week. My success wasn't because I knew more or worked harder than anyone else. My success was that I built a brand. The brand had nothing to do with the real estate agency I was working for. The brand was me. My brand was selling my loyalty, efficiency and effectiveness to my clients. I built new networks based upon my initial network and I continue to build that network today. More than 50% of my clients are repeats and referrals from other clients. Building my brand and my network has been a continual reinvestment in my business. There are several key factors that I have learned from years of experience:*

1. Always seek to discover and understand my client's needs and expectation, realizing my job is to sell their home or help them to buy a home.

2. Know what matters to my clients. I keep a detailed portfolio

or profile of every client. I know about their family, their kids and things that matter to them. Every conversation is a learning opportunity about my clients. I want them to know that I care about them and that the sale or purchase of a home is the most important thing in their life that moment.

3. The sale or purchase of a home is an on-going process that ends when the client thinks the process is over, not merely when all the papers are signed. I can't tell you how often my repeat clients recall little things I did to help their transition from one home to another.

4. My clients know that the sales transaction is a team effort. I'm the mother of 10 kids. My husband and the entire family are football fanatics. When I'm working with a family to buy or sell a home, I'm the quarterback. I study the situation and I'm prepared to lead the team. I'm prepared for the success and failures that can come with the buying and selling of a home. A great sales person has to study. Your knowledge is the differentiator.

5. My goal is to ensure that my clients know that there is no substitute for what I offer. Even on the occasions when a client is relocating out of my area, I know I'm successful when they call me for advice. Giving that advice is assurance that I will be at the top of the list when someone asks them if they know a great agent in Chicago.

What Mary Ann Falkenberg advises is the key of a SAM. Creating the real or perceived idea that there is no substitute for your expertise will be an incredible advantage for current and future sales. There will always be similar, high quality products but your differentiation strategy takes quality and your integrity to a significantly higher level. The business gains an advantage in the market as customers view your product as unique because of the value your personal service contributes.

No Limit to What You Can Offer: Find the Competitive Edge

Whether you're a business owner or a member of the sales force at your company, the concept of gaining a competitive edge is your willingness to invest the time and effort to becoming the best. Again, YOU are your business and your business is YOU. We all have direct competition; gaining the edge is what separates you from being average versus being a SAM:

1. First and foremost invest in YOU, sharpen your skillset. Be willing to spend the dollars and time to make sure you gain ROI: a return on your investment.

2. Do basic research and development. Buy your competitor's products or do some reconnaissance on their services. Study it, dissect it, and assess its strengths and weaknesses so that you can devise a better presentation of your own product or service (even if you determine that your competitor's product is better than yours).

3. Create a recognizable distinction between you and your competitor by not relying on "cookie cutter" models for your sales and marketing strategies.

"Gorilla" Marketing Before its Time

In my younger days as a 24 year old I had no fear and I was full of ideas. I mentioned previously my work in the health and fitness industry, working with my mentor Al Philips and franchise owner Arnold Schwarzenegger, building the World Gyms in downtown Chicago. This was an incredible opportunity. I was young and wanted not only to be successful, but to make an impression on my mentor and the industry. At the time, our logo was a gorilla. I had a crazy idea that I knew would separate us from our competition, was given the green light, but was told to do it at my own risk and expense. I took some of my staff and hired homeless people and put them to work. I put them in gorilla costumes in the dead of winter, gave them World Gym flyers and strategically placed them at every train station to market our gym to the public. Not only did I increase the traffic at our gyms, I sold more memberships and exceeded all projections. The whole thing became a media sensation; a plus. Pictures were taken by the Sears Tower and the headlines read "Gorillas Invade Chicago!" The lesson here is that I made the investment, I knew how the other gyms were marketing their services and I created a competitive distinction that allowed our facility to blow away the competition. I acted like an entrepreneur, not an employee.

My Mentor Al Philips with Arnold Schwarzenegger working out at the gym in Chicago.

***

Real "Gorilla Marketing" at its Best!

Anyone who has done business with me has one of my "The Main Man" or "The Big Cheese" bobble-heads, created in my likeness and representative of one of my personas. What a crazy, humorous and, most of all, memorable way to get my clients to take notice and remember me. Accompanied by my 1-800-MAINMAN and 1-800-BIGCHEESE phone numbers, my marketing machine is well oiled and high performing. My motto is, "Even if you don't buy from me today, you'll always remember me tomorrow!" And I marked my territory like a pit bull by sending a bobble to every prospective and current client. That's reinvestment in ME and my business! That's creating distinction and gaining competitive edge at its best!

That's how I was able to build one of the largest mortgage companies in South Florida and become the largest Italian cheese salesperson in the USA; by getting my customers to remember me not only as Anthony Caliendo, but as an icon. My bobbles make a statement and an impression on my customers and allowed me to open more doors and most certainly close more accounts.

Reinvestment in YOU is essential. It takes risk, it takes creativity. It means coming up with the right formula and right strategy. Making the investment in you and creating a distinction is KEY to becoming a SAM!

"If you don't drive your business you will be driven out of business."[39]
—B.C. Forbes

***

"If you don't buy from me today, you'll always remember me tomorrow."

39   Tan, Henry, 2013. ProGood. http://progood.me/3348/b-c-forbes-if-you-dont-drive-your-business

Lessons From the Ultimate Sales Assassin Master:

1. **No Limit to What You Can Be:** There is no limit to what you can be. Your limit is only your imagination, your vision and your willingness to step outside of your comfort zone.

2. **Learn from Dr. Seuss: Words That Differentiate You[40]:**

   a. "Today you are You, that is truer than true. There is no one alive who is "Youer" than You."—Dr. Seuss

   b. "You have brains in your head. You have feet in your shoes. You can steer yourself in any direction you choose. You're on your own, and you know what you know. And you are the guy who'll decide where to go."—Dr. Seuss

   c. "Think left, think right, think low, and think high. Oh, the thinks you can think up if only you try!"—Dr. Seuss

   d. "You're off to Great Places! Today is your day! Your mountain is waiting, So... get on your way!"—Dr. Seuss

3. **Differentiating You and Your Business Is Reinventing What You Offer in Relationship to the Competition:** This means creating a new vision and possessing the ability to communicate a New Value Proposition—why you're better, or different, than your competitors. It means finding the formula for business sustainability.

4. **Be "The World's Leading Expert":** A SAM works each day to be the ultimate expert. The word expert defines you as different, the best and one with more knowledge than anyone else. Your product or service may be the same as

---

40   Goodreads, https://www.goodreads.com/author/quotes/61105.Dr_Seuss

everyone else's, but as the expert, you know more than the competition. Customers love working with the best. Therefore, earn the distinction, and use your new found distinction to set yourself apart.

With your expert status, you are ready to declare YOU as a brand along with your product or service. At this point, your expertise, including your personality, education and life experiences, becomes integral to the package you offer. These items should all be included in your quest to stand out from your competition. Your abilities should be unparalleled in your market. Invest in yourself, learn, mold and shape yourself. Declare yourself the expert and prove you are the expert and the ultimate SAM.

Sales Assassin Personal Development

Defining and Realizing Opportunities for Your Reinvestment

We defined *reinvestment* as the individual ways that you make positive change in your personal entrepreneurial development in both the simplest and most complex ways. The following questions will assist you in laying out a plan for your own personal development.

1. Define specific opportunities for you to invest in your personal and/or professional development.

   _____

   _____

   _____

2. Identify barriers to your reinvestment opportunities that could make it impossible for you to achieve success in the next three months.

   a. Define the key barriers to your success.

   _____

   b. What steps could you take in preparation to address the barriers defined?

   _____

3. What are the risks associated with your approach to reinvestment?

   _____

4. What is the potential ROI (return on your investment) if you invest in your development?

   _____

CHAPTER 9

SAM BELT 8: LESSONS OF LIFE

Wisdom from Anthony Caliendo, the Ultimate Sales Assassin

The ability to overcome failure is our ability to embrace the chance to learn—the challenge to demonstrate Passion, Dedication and Courage

THE FAILURES I'VE had in my life have been painful. They challenged me and my family.

Success and failure are inevitable lessons of life. Our failure can be very expensive in terms of dollars, confidence, physical and mental pain. However, it is the belts of SAM success that will assist you in overcoming failure. Yes, our mistakes and failures are necessary parts of life and yes, mistakes and failures can be expensive. In life and especially in sales our mistakes, shortcomings and errors in judgment are learning experiences. These are the Life Lessons. We each have an ample supply of these experiences. A broken bone, if given the right care, will mend or fuse stronger than it was originally. The lessons derived from our life experiences are the same. Your life experiences, the good, the bad and the ugly make you stronger and smarter.

***

"In essence, if we want to direct our lives, we must take control of our consistent actions. It's not what we do once in a while that shapes our lives, but what we do consistently."
—Tony Robbins

***

Lessons In Life Are Vehicles of Change

The lessons you learn from life allow and demand you to change and adapt to situations and circumstances. Life's lessons are powerful and rapidly become the foundation for your success. But you have to understand how to absorb these lessons and use them as a vehicle to become a Sales Assassin and then be able sustain Sales Assassin performance success. Sustainable performance is difficult for anyone regardless of your professional calling. There are two drivers that allow you to sustain performance at consistently high levels:

1. **Use Passion as a Source of Energy:** As I said in SAM Belt PDC, passion is the sensation of feeling driven to success. When you have the passion for your work, your work then rewards you with increased energy and enthusiasm for more work. The greater benefit is that the energy becomes contagious and a continuous fuel source in your best and worst of times.

2. **Continuously Absorb Knowledge and Information:** The other source of fuel for sustainable performance requires your mind to be willing to learn and use what you have learned in the most effective way. Remember, you will learn

from your successes and from your failures. When you learn and attain more knowledge, you continuously grow in the belief of what you can do and what you can be. Knowledge makes you strong and this strength gives you the ability to sustain. Just like energy, knowledge is contagious.

Passion for your work and continuous absorption of knowledge gives you harmony in your professional and personal life. This passion provides you the momentum to overcome the adversities you face and give you the energy to challenge the difficult odds against success. The Sales Assassin searches for passion and searches for opportunities to learn. Without these tools your sales work becomes routine, the same old thing each and everyday. The combination of passion and absorption of knowledge drives a SAM to achieve greatness. Greatness becomes a relentless challenge that you want to achieve. It feeds the mind, your body and your spirit.

Life lessons must become your vehicle for change, your vehicle to excel after the disappointments and the failures that are inevitable in life. The old cliché says, "The only constant is change." Success in sales is learning from life experiences and the constant changes that our customers and environment demand of us. Life's lessons are your ability as a SAM to not only adapt to change that a sales life demands, but more importantly to be facilitator and leader of your own change vehicle. Your change vehicle is the ability to know when to shift gears.

- Danger = Change Your Gear
- Competition = Change Your Approach
- Customers = Change Your Style

Don't even attempt to be a SAM if you aren't willing to change based on the experiences you have had, and the learning you can get from others who have valuable experience. Don't tell me you don't have the time or the willingness to change. If you can't find the time or the will to change how you do things you can't ever expect to be anything more than average. A SAM has no time or patience for the average or mediocre. People change for one of two reasons:

1. Something or someone forced you to change—you reacted to circumstances.

2. You were looking for opportunity to grow—you anticipated circumstances.

***

Wisdom from Anthony Caliendo, the Ultimate Sales Assassin

Life Can Teach You Many Things, But You Have To Be Willing To Learn

If you're not willing to learn, hang it up folks. Some of you will read this book and you'll get the message and start learning immediately from the SAM approach. You will engage a strategy to improve your sales performance and you will welcome life lessons to provide continual learning opportunities. You will reach back in time and recall experiences that left both good and bad impressions. Your impressions will be logged in your brain and unleashed when you need them and when you least expect it. My friends, your life lessons are powerful tools and investments you have made in yourself. Success is always a result of the accumulation of knowledge. This knowledge is turned into skills, which you put in place with a strategy to translate your new skills and knowledge into sales success.

One of the difficult challenges you face is the desire to place fault for negative experiences on others or on circumstances beyond your control. Some things are beyond your control but even in these cases, there is so much to learn. You have to have the ability to separate out the "BS," hold yourself accountable for achieving success, and manage the challenges. Most of the life lessons come from decisions that you made. Your decisions are your choices and you own these choices: you have to move forward and learn from your bad choices.

Here are three of my Life Lessons that have been invaluable learning experiences:

Life Lesson 101: Egg Cartons and Beer

When I was 9 years old my family lived near a golf course. Even at that young age, I saw an opportunity to make some cash. I would fish the golf balls from the lake and bushes, take them home, clean them up, put them in egg cartons and re-sell them to the golfers. One day I decided, why not add my famous Caliendo Lemonade to the menu. One of the golfers said, "Hey Kid, now all you need to do is sell some beers and you'll be in business!" The light bulb turned on. I didn't realize at the time that that golfer was making the suggestion in jest, or was he? So I went home, took the beers from the fridge and proceeded to sell Golf Balls, Caliendo's Lemonade, and Ice Cold Beers. Four days later I was banned from the golf course.

The Life Lessons I Learned:

- You can create opportunity from nothing and turn it into something.

- Observe: when, where and what need exists: now fill the need.

- Innovate and Create: keep building, keep creating, and now let your customers tell you what they love and desire.

- Who is the potential customer: decide what customers have money to spend, have the desire to spend, and are looking for the opportunity to buy.

- Create the right value proposition for what you have to offer: success is a meeting of the minds between you and your customer.

- The competition knows a good thing when they see it and might just want a piece of the action.

- Risk-taking must be a part of SAM success. However, uncalculated risks are not necessarily the right course of action, especially if it stands to ruin a good thing.

Lesson in Life 102: World Gym-Dream Deferred

In my early years I was in the health club business. I had a mentor, Al Philips, Chicago's guru in the health club business. I would have followed this guy anywhere. At that time, I left Bally's to pursue building up the Arnold Schwarzenegger's World Gyms alongside my mentor. I was flattered that he handpicked me to build this dream with him. The deal was sweetened with an incentive to earn a small percentage of the profits after I successfully built the first two locations. I exceeded all my expectations and Al's as well. I was a leader in pre-sales. Memberships increased and I managed the construction of our second location, ironically right on the Chicago River down from the Chicago Stock Exchange where I would soon work. Receiving a percentage of the profits didn't work out and yes I was disappointed and angry. I'm not suggesting that my mentor did a bait and switch. The fact was that our profitability had not been realized and that was a legitimate reason. In hindsight, I should have kept steadfast, but at the time, my young ego and relentless ambition would not allow me to accept that rationale. I respected my mentor, but I put in my resignation. My youth and arrogance got the best of me. Time to move on from the greatest business that I'd known at that point in my life. God, did I have the passion for this job. However, I looked down the Chicago River towards the Chicago Mercantile Exchange (CME) and left the health club business forever.

The Life Lessons I Learned:

- Learn when to cut your losses and move on to bigger things and other dreams.

- Know what you're worth, believe in yourself and make a decision not to live another person's dreams.

- Loyalty is great, but don't be loyal to a fault.

- Integrity and trust matter: Make sure your name is a synonym for integrity and trust.

Life Lesson 103: Face the Inevitable, Then Salvage and Regroup

By 2005 I was known in the South Florida mortgage industry as "The Main Man." I'd built a self-sustaining, colossal operation with four offices and a staff of over 100 mortgage professionals. In mid-2007 the South Florida mortgage implosion began and the housing boom busted. When the economy collapsed, my mortgage business fell right in the toilet with everyone else's. I had to put out fires on a daily basis. I started changing my then famous radio ads and talk to the South Florida community about the crisis they were facing as homeowners. No matter what I did, the results were minimal at best. If you were in the housing industry during that time, you know what I mean. Appraisals weren't being accepted, lenders were closing their doors and forcing us to try to find new lenders, my brokers were trying to survive with less money in their pockets because the business just wasn't paying anymore. A business death can be quick and painful. Every day I tried to breathe new life into an unresponsive economy. My CPR efforts and electro-shock therapy introduced no new life into my business. I was forced to close my offices one by one until I had nothing left.

My Mortgage Company's slogan was "Our Fees Are Cut in ½"

The Life Lessons I Learned:

- Just like the Titanic, as much as you would like to save a sinking ship, you can't stop it from going to the bottom of the ocean. In other words, you can't stop the inevitable;

you can only try to salvage the wreckage.

- Transition, regrouping and re-direction are necessary.

- Now is the time to believe in yourself. Reinvent yourself and believe. Believe that you can pick up and start over again.

"Never give up on what you really want to do. The person with big dreams is more powerful than one with all the facts."[41]
—Albert Einstein

***

Lessons in Life: A Flea Market Full of Lessons

Not far from where I live there is a famous flea market outside of Ft. Lauderdale. These markets are crazy places to buy and sell, and watch in amazement how people negotiate on both sides of the transaction. As much as I dread the crowds, I always enjoy the real-life education in human behavior that I get at a flea market. This is a different breed of people. People who simply buy and sell stuff. People start arriving at 7 a.m. The earlier you are the better stuff, the later you are the better the deal. I park my butt on a bench next to a couple booths of complete junk and start watching the art of Flea Market Salesmanship at work while my wife and kids amber up and down the aisle looking for stuff.

The first wave of activity starts: a woman and her daughter come up to the booth holding a couple items. The first, a pair of small lamps with a slight crack in one. The second, an old belt a bit worn, but a cool looking belt buckle that looked tarnished but could be

---

41   Block, Lindsey, 2013. 10 Inspiring Life Lesson & 5 Quotes via Albert Einstein, http://www.elephantjournal.com/2013/01/10-inspiring-life-lessons-via-albert-einstein/

polished. "How much you want for these?" she asks. "Oh, I don't know…how about $25 for the belt and $50 for the lamps?" he responded. "For this cracked lamp and this beat up old belt?" she says. He says, "What do you want to give me?" "Ten for the belt and $30 for the lamps" she says. "I just can't do that. I make nothing off this stuff. I know the lamp has a crack, but it's a set and you never find this type of carving. I bought the set for $70 a week ago without the crack. I cracked it this morning. That buckle is worth $25 and a little leather oil will make it really cool with a white blouse," said the old flea marketer, as I wonder why on earth she wants this junk. He then said, "Ok, here's what I will do. I'll give you both for $50." I laughed to myself, as her daughter says, "Mom, that belt would be really cool with your jeans skirt and cowboy boots." She pulled out a credit card to pay. At that moment the old guy said, "Ok that's $50 plus $5 for the credit card charge." Amazing, she just paid $50 for 2 things worth nothing, well ok, worth $20 and paid another $5 to use her credit card. What a racket.

Sales Observation 1: It's amazing what people will buy. There is a market for everything and someone is always willing to overpay.

Sales Observation 2: Negotiation is an art form that you can learn with time. You have to remember no matter how good you think you are there is someone else who is a better, more experienced negotiator. By the way never let'em see you sweat. You gotta love Kenny Roger's advice:

> *"You've got to know when to hold 'em*
> *Know when to fold 'em*
> *Know when to walk away*
> *Know when to run*
> *You never count your money*

When you're sittin' at the table
There'll be time enough for countin'
When the dealin's done.

Lessons from the Ultimate Sales Assassin:

1. Our failure can be very expensive in terms of dollars, confidence, physical and mental pain. However, it is the belts of SAM success that will assist you in overcoming failure.

2. The lessons you learn from life allow and demand you to change and adapt to situations and circumstances. Life's lessons are powerful and rapidly become the foundation for your success.

3. Learn when to cut your losses and move on to bigger things and other dreams. Know what you're worth, believe in yourself and make a decision not to live another person's dreams. Loyalty is great, but don't be loyal to a fault.

CHAPTER 10

SAM BELT 9: LIFESTYLE CHANGE

WHO ARE YOU? Do you have a clue what you want to be? Do you have a clue as to what you can be? Are you a sales person because you desire it—live and breath it? Or are you a sales person because you haven't been successful in any other career path? If you don't have answers to these questions you have not achieved SAM level performance. SAM requires an understanding of the person you are. No one else can tell you. It is a process of self-discovery.

***

Wisdom from Anthony Caliendo, the Ultimate Sales Assassin

I seldom find sales people who grew up and went to college seeing sales as their great career choice.

Facing the Facts

As the Ultimate Sales Assassin Master, there are several points that I need to make:

1. You WILL NOT become a SAM by merely reading this book.

2. Memorizing the names of the 9 Belts and their main concepts will not guarantee you SAM status.

3. You will not transform overnight and emerge the next morning with your SAM suit on.

Becoming a Sales Assassin Master means making a mental and emotional commitment to completely changing your behaviors and the way you think, act and react to situations. It's about replacing bad habits with positive ideas, concepts and new habits. Not just any concepts, ideas and habits, but those that have a dynamic impact on your journey to becoming more successful in sales and in life. This is the part in this book where you now must decide whether or not you're truly committed to the journey of change, the creation of your own ideas and concepts that enable success and allow you to pass the test of SAM life. This is a journey of the self-discovery of your capabilities and to your ability to find the outrageous opportunities, using outrageous differentiated thoughts and ideas.

During and after reading this book, I know that some of you will have real moments of reflection and self-discovery. Some will walk away validated in that they're already putting a lot of my concepts into good practice and only have a few things they need to focus on to elevate them to the next level. However, others will walk away feeling completely overwhelmed with the realization that they have many behaviors and attitudes that require focus and change. Both of these realizations require deep commitment and concentration on making lasting and permanent changes; lifestyle changes!

Lifestyle changes require making the choices needed to achieve and sustain desired results. Making the right choices means having the right attitude. Having the right attitude means making conscious decisions about how you want to think and react in order to achieve the best outcomes possible. These changes, choices, attitudes and decisions must be repetitive changes, choices, attitudes and decisions and not just acts; they must become intrinsic reactions and habits. In order to become a SAM, you must not accept mediocrity. Every concept that you learn in my book must be put into action to become a SAM. That means you cannot accept being average. It means you must have the desire and the will to make the lifestyle changes necessary for success and Sales Assassin Mastery!

In life there are several factors that drive real change. Sometimes change is born from chaos or from growing weary of bad circumstances. Sometimes change is a preemptive strike. I say that the changes you need to make in order to become a SAM are a combination of both. Circle back to the Introduction of this book when I introduced my SAM philosophy. Determining what lifestyle changes you must make in order to drive your SAM transformation starts with asking yourself hard and honest questions about your character, your personality, your values, your habits and then evaluating the successes (or lack thereof) you've had in sales so far. And at the conclusion of your self-discovery process, you'll come to a fork in the road. Decide now: are you going to stay on the path of least resistance and accept mediocrity? Or are you going to step up to the plate and stop making excuses?

All of my students choose the path to becoming a SAM; a big welcome to those of you who have decided to join us. No, you're not a SAM yet but congratulations on making this life changing decision; the decision to strive towards being in the top 1%; the commitment to true mental and physical challenge and sacrifice.

Now that you've read about what a SAM is and how I became a SAM, what's next?

Maintain Your Motivation

The biggest challenge you're going to face on this journey is being able to maintain your motivation—being able to keep the flame alive each day geared toward continuous improvement and personal growth. Anyone who has ever attempted to make impactful changes has struggled with how to stay on target in order to achieve his or her goals. The best proof and example of this is New Year's Resolutions. Since I'm Italian and a Roman Gladiator at heart, I love the fact that New Year's Resolutions actually began in ancient Rome when citizens made promises to the god Janus (for whom the month January is named) at the beginning of each new year. This custom carried on to modern times and today adults make promises to themselves at the beginning of each year to make certain lifestyle changes. Research indicates that the top three resolutions are:

1. Physical and mental health related
   a. Lose weight
   b. Stop smoking
   c. Be more positive
2. Financially related
   a. Cease bad spending habits
   b. Release from debt
3. Career related
   a. Obtain a better job

    b. Do better at the current job

    c. Establish your own business

According to statistics, 45% of Americans make New Year's Resolutions (so over 141,000,000 people). Only 8% are successful in achieving them. What? Even worse, almost ½ of these people can't even keep their resolutions past January! Why is this happening? Are we making wrong or unrealistic resolutions? Are we without willpower? Are we allowing our emotions or temptations to take over? But realize, statistics also show that 52% of Americans that make resolutions go into it with the utmost of confidence and best intentions in the beginning. So why the alarming failure rate? Perhaps we just aren't committed to making the changes. If you're not committed to the change, then there is no motivation to work toward results; there's no spark and certainly there is no flame to keep alive.

Your challenge: keeping the flame alive each day and staying committed to your task. In sales, as in life, a strong way to stay motivated and in tune with the changes you need to make is by positive reinforcement that comes from supportive, positive people. This makes up the basis of your SAM support system. If you constantly have negative, unsupportive people in your atmosphere who perpetually extinguish your fire, turn them off as quickly as humanly possible! Notice that celebrities and other prominent, successful people say this all the time, and it's true. Who you surround yourself with and allow to influence you makes the biggest impact on the direction you will ultimately travel. Obviously, there are some conditions that we simply cannot control, i.e. unconstructive or unproductive people at work that we have to interact with in some form or another. The key is to find a way to mitigate the negative noise and refrain from feeding into whatever brand of negativity they release. Get yourself around positive, infectious people. Channel their positive energy, try to emulate them. Be likable and become infectiously positive yourself. Become someone else's positive reinforcement. Bring a buddy into your SAM support system. Realize, ultimately only you can change you and you are responsible for creating your own positive reinforcement and channeling your own positive energy. You are going to have setbacks and moments of weakness; that's normal. But when the SAM mentality kicks in, you will have the power to recover and get back on the path. Train and condition yourself to this end; that is having the resolve to recover and refocus. In the end, it's all on you; however, having that support team to keep you both motivated and accountable is one of the keys to keeping your flame alive while on this journey to becoming a SAM. In his book The Laws of the Ring, former UFC Champion Urijah Faber states,

"There are many times when we need to stand on our own and make big decisions that can dictate the course of our passion. I relate it to the big fight: I enter the cage with the people from my corner— trainers and coaches—but when the bell rings I'm left alone to make decisions based on the teachings of the community."[42]

SAM Lifestyle Change ties directly into SAM Mindset. As you begin to develop the SAM Mindset (learning to control Mind Rollercoaster Phenomenon [MRP] and mentally committing to controlling your responses and reactions), lifestyle changes will begin to emerge and take shape on their own. In sales, you harness positive energy and keep your flame alive when you're on a roll making close after close, sales after sale, and score after score. Yes, the rewards are real, the endorphins sky-rocket, the money is being made and gratification

---

42   http://www.amazon.com/Laws-Ring-Urijah-Faber/dp/B00B9ZF0HI

keeps your flame alive. But what happens when the numbers are down? Remember, I discussed how a SAM isn't defeated from setbacks; he or she refuels his tank from them and vows to work ten times as hard when circumstances go backwards. You know you're on the path to becoming a SAM and making real lifestyle changes when you can use the lows to your advantage. A SAM automatically emerges from the lows and anticipates the next peak when he or she is in a valley. Use this skill as you continue on this journey to making lifestyle changes.

Your mind, body and spirit must be synchronized if you want to make all of the changes necessary for success. That means accepting that mental, physical and emotional development is key to your business and sales success. They're all interrelated. You can't have one without the other. You cannot be successful in sales if you don't have a positive mental, physical and emotional identity. Okay, so some of us have bigger egos than others. But having a good sense of your identity and having a good opinion of yourself is essential to being a success in anything you do!

There are several lifestyle changes that can be made in order to boost your sense of identity. When you feel better about who you are and your capabilities, you will perform better and you will see positive results. It can be as simple as paying more attention to your outward appearance because perception is reality in the sales business. If you look successful and present yourself as successful, you will be perceived as successful.

I'm the Ultimate SAM, I'm The Main Man, and I'm The Cheese Boss. But I'm also known as "The Suit." In the Italian cheese business, I typically exhibit at about ten food tradeshows per year, nationally and internationally. Picture it; I'm in a 2,000,000 sq. foot convention center with 1,000 or so exhibitors and under the same roof are about 50 of my biggest Italian cheese competitors. Approximately 10,000 buyers are in attendance visiting each booth and making snap decisions on which companies deserve their time and which ones do not. I don't get a second chance to make a first impression. Besides having one of the best, most attractive and visually appealing booths in the building, I make sure that my personal appearance screams success, professionalism and confidence. So when I'm glad-handing hundreds of buyers whose business I want, they might not necessarily remember my name when I'm done, but they remember my style, they remember me as "The Suit." They remember how well I represented myself, my company and my products and now I'm a shoe-in for the follow up. This personal appearance is part of my lifestyle and my brand.

Again, the lifestyle changes you need to make in order to become a SAM have to be impactful and they have to coincide with your journey to becoming more successful in sales. Start by identifying true lifestyle changes you need to make based on the 9 Belts. Be precise, make them visual by writing them down and make a plan of attack that you can put into motion each and every day. Then, go to work with the Eye of the Tiger. It took Apollo Creed to remind Rocky that in order to regain his rank, he needed to retrain his mindset and focus on the challenge. The lyrics say ***"Rising up to the challenge of our rival."***[43] That's you, you're Rocky (and I'm Apollo Creed) and in order to gain rank, you need to change your inner-self that will ultimately put you at the top of your game and outsell your competitors! And remember, your mindset to make these changes begins when you go to bed the night before, allowing

---

43   Elyrics.net. http://www.elyrics.net/read/g/green-day-lyrics/eye-of-the-tiger-lyrics.html

you to awake with a renewed sense of optimism and purpose. The transformation will take shape and you will become a SAM!

6 Steps to Lifestyle Change

Making lifestyle changes can be challenging, even if you have made changes before. If you are like me you have tried and failed on countless occasions to make these seemingly simple adjustments in your daily or weekly routines. The problem is that most of us have no idea of what we are getting into when we decide we need to make a change.

Here are six essential steps that will teach you more about what makes us tick and how to make important lifestyle changes.

1. *Identify Your Priorities and Commitments*

Establishing priorities and changing behaviors go hand in hand. If you focus on the behavior without determining the priorities, the behavior will always revert back. The first thing to do is to identify your priorities. This is really a matter of making a list of what is important to you (e.g., family, work, health, etc.) and then organizing these things in order of importance. With this list you are more aware of your priorities than you were before. If this causes you to want to change your priorities, this is an important step toward making a lifestyle change. Remember, if you change your priorities, the behavior changes will follow.

People often say, "My problem is not priorities, it is lack of commitment." So what's the difference? The real question: are you spending the most time on the things that are most important to you? If you doubt that your behavior is reflecting your priorities and instead feel that you simply lack commitment, then ask yourself why you think you are spending more time on something that is not so important to you. Does that make sense?

2. Become Aware of Your Belief System

Your priorities are determined by your belief system, and your belief system is based on the culture in which you have been raised, your life experiences and the conscious choices you make. A SAM realizes that the past does not dictate the present or the future. If you look at the sources of your beliefs or behaviors, you will realize that most of them exist because of an experience you have had or lessons you learned from past experiences. If you realize that this belief or behavior is holding you back, you must ask yourself why you continue to believe or behave in this manner. This belief or behavior may have served you well at one time, but is it serving the same purpose today and will it serve the same purpose in the future?

The more you are aware of what you truly believe the more likely you are to make the choices and behave in the manner that gives you the needed ROI on your time and efforts. If you want your lifestyle to change then you must be ready to change you, change your beliefs and be willing to self-discover a new foundation. This is a core SAM belief.

3. Create an Individualized Strategy

If you haven't figured it out the one-size-fits-all approach to life doesn't work. We are all individuals, meaning we are unique, possessing differences that are valuable to us as humans.

Your goal must be to determine which life strategies work best for you. This depends as much on your life experiences and the way you were raised as it does on your ability and willingness to adhere to new ideas and concepts to which you are exposed. It has been my experience that a SAM will not make a lifestyle change unless they feel it is right or it makes sense, and is clearly linked to and supports whatever goals they have set for themselves. The institutions of our world such as religions, governments and politics—are based on a set of beliefs. If you practice any one particular religion or political affiliation, you chose it because—based on all the information available to you—it made sense to you or because it feels right in your heart and your mind.

A SAM is not afraid to create his individualized life strategy for achieving success. If you build a life strategy, you will most likely adhere to it and achieve success.

4. *Find Your Passion—Dedication—Courage, Then Motivate Yourself*

I spoke early in this book about Passion, Dedication and Courage as a set of strong emotions and confidence that will move you past your comfort area—the area that most often brings you to a screeching halt. You should realize that it is with PDC that your belief system will flourish and will drive you through to achieve your personal lifestyle strategy. It is now time to find motivation and stay motivated. Motivation is the process that initiates, guides and maintains your goal-oriented behaviors. Motivation drives you to act—motivation drives you to achieve—motivation drives you to overcome—motivation drives you to go forward when your mind and body want to say no. Motivation is the force inside of you that activates your behavior.

There are three major elements to motivation: activation, persistence and intensity. **Activation** is the decision to initiate a behavior, such as deciding to go after a new element of business or a new customer. **Persistence** is your continued effort to go after this new client even though obstacles may exist, such as substantial competition that is going after the same client. Finally, **intensity** is the force and fierceness you use to take on the challenge. It is your level of concentration and vitality that goes into pursuing your goal to gain that new client.

"Things do not happen; things are made to happen."[44]
—John F. Kennedy

***

5. *Success: See It—Touch It—Feel It—Live It*

How do you feel when you achieve those great moments in your life? When you have overcome all the obstacles and you have success in your hands. In those moments, you come alive and live in that moment.

Many studies have demonstrated that the ability to visually see success is an extremely effective tool used by professional athletes, celebrities, millionaires, and other successful people in all walks of life. The greatest path to success is your ability to visualize it before it comes together. Athletes always think about the big play or the perfect shot they see in their mind before the moment actually happens. They rehearse those moments of success and greatness over and over in their

---

44   Kennedy, John, 1963. http://und.edu/john-f-kennedy-digital-archive/delivered.php

minds. They dream of being the hero of the moment and relish in a vision of success. Actors write their acceptance speech just in case they actually win the award: they're prepared for their success.

There are many reasons why visualization is so effective— it allows you to find the emotional elements of your determination and is a way of implanting success within your subconscious mind. Carl Jung was a great psychologist of the late 19th century. He talked about visualization of success as your unconscious mind communicating with your conscious mind through pictures or images, not through words. This visualization is locked in your mind and can then be easily recalled whenever you want or need to see it again. Your visualization serves as an inspiration and then your motivation. For the SAM they can **See It—Touch It— Feel It, Then They Will Achieve It and Live It.**

6. *Make Decisions—Make Commitments and Live With Them*

Life is about the decisions you make and living with the ramifications of those decisions. Keep in mind that your decisions should be viewed as commitments that come from your heart. You cannot simplify the difficulty in making your decision to change. There is no question that you have the power to change. The question is whether you have the will, dedication, motivation and courage to change. Is success tied to those of us who decide to succeed? If you want your lifestyle to change, then you must change you and your self-image. Your self-image is the reflection that you see in the mirror. Get serious about your commitment to yourself. If you don't like what you see then change now. It's your choice.

In the beginning of this chapter, I used the New Year's Resolution analogy. If your New Year's Resolution didn't start January 1st, then start it today. There is no time to wait and procrastination is not your friend. I want this book to reach the millions of sales professionals who are specifically yearning to improve their circumstances. Consider this your SAM Year of Evolution! Putting all of the lessons from the Ultimate SAM into action will drive you toward true lifestyle change and evolution into Sales Assassin Mastery.

Lessons from the Ultimate Sales Assassin

1. Becoming a Sales Assassin Master means making a mental and emotional commitment to completely change your behaviors and the way you think, act and react to situations.
2. Lifestyle changes involve making the choices needed to achieve and sustain desired results. Making the right choices means having the right attitude.
3. In sales as in life, to stay motivated and in tune with the changes you need to make is by positive reinforcement that comes from within yourself and from supportive, positive people.

CONCLUSIONS

DISCOVER YOUR SAM DISTINCTIVE NATURE TO ACHIEVE

THIS BOOK HAS provided a comprehensive look at a series of skills and concepts to control, mold and shape your **SAM Distinctive Nature to Achieve**—your SAM DNA. Your success and ability to achieve **Sales Assassin Excellence** must be grounded and framed in your personal motivation. SAM DNA is your achievement motivation and your mindset that leads your need to set realistic challenging goals and achieve your sales goals.

I have demanded of you a shift in the philosophy around the sales process that corporations and sales professionals engage each day. I have challenged the traditional sales philosophy that teaches you basic concepts, like getting to work early and being the last to leave will help you improve your work ethic. I have challenged you to change your direction to a more comprehensive sales approach that begins where the other philosophies end. I have taught you how to redefine yourself providing guidance for self-improvement, not only as a salesperson, but also as an individual. You have learned that even with all the tools and the best sales philosophy and process, success is only achieved when you have the ability to stand in front of the mirror each day and declare to yourself:

*"I am a Sales Assassin Master and I will achieve sales success today and everyday and I deserve and will achieve prosperity. I have the **Passion, Dedication and Courage** to achieve perfection in my craft. I have found my own **Distinctive Nature to Achieve**. My DNA is my own unique and distinctive self. I am special, creative and powerful."*

"I am the Greatest. I said that even before I knew I was."
—Muhammad Ali

You must remember that sales books have traditionally talked about a sales strategy as a plan that hopefully puts a company and its products in a position to gain a competitive advantage. These strategies supposedly help organizations and you focus on potential customers and communicate with them in a way that is meaningful and drives sales results. The idea has been that all you need to know is how products or services can solve customer problems. Then all you have to do is focus on four things:

1. Find and identify potential customers
2. Qualify customers
3. Make a proposal
4. Close the sale

Yes, I agree that these 4 points are your starting point, but to be a SAM there is so much more to learn and experience. You have to find your sales DNA—Again Find Your Distinctive Nature to Achieve! This book has taken you beyond the 4 traditional elements of life in the sales industry. The central challenge that I have posed to you is:

How do you develop the desire to make the changes necessary to adopt the SAM sales model? How do you find your SAM: Distinctive Nature to Achieve?

The search for your SAM DNA requires that you:

1. Figure out if you really like what you do.

2. Determine if you believe in sales as a viable career for you; or are you in a sales job because you have failed at other careers.

3. Determine if your personality, your life style and your ways of thinking are suited for a career in sales.

4. Determine if you can become passionate about your career each day and especially when the economy is tough.

5. Determine what changes you must make in order to drive your success and determine if these changes will be impactful enough to begin your transformation process.

The sales professional who possess the right DNA has a strong desire to be successful in the most important elements of life, and he is gratified from the success achieved when faced with the most demanding challenges. Therefore, the SAM is energized and willing to expend intense effort over long timespans in the pursuit of his goals.

A SAM cannot avoid the failures of life. Those who avoid failure become focused on protecting themselves from the embarrassment and sense of incompetence that can accompany the moments when success is not achieved.

On the contrary, a SAM will not take the easy path or the less rewarding challenges. Instead, they find strength within themselves, always searching and shaping one's mindset through the proper mental and physical preparation. The SAM knows that our DNA does not come from a vacuum, but is associated with an elaborate assortment of beliefs that justify the commitment to intense effort toward sales achievement. The core beliefs that differentiate those with the SAM DNA are those who know and embrace:

1. **Success driven by a personal and professional commitment**

   The SAM believes that personal and professional initiative, desire, and tenacity are key determinants of success at demanding tasks.

2. **Demanding SMARTS goals are opportunities**

   The SAM sales professional accepts demanding goals where success may not be certain. For the professional who avoids failure, they will find themselves seeing the most challenging goals as a threat and potential for failure. Rest assured that the SAM with the right DNA will declare to all "the greatest challenges give us the greatest rewards in life".

3. **The search for achievement and success is enjoyable and has value**

   The SAM links the effort it takes to achieve success on the most demanding goals with Passion, Dedication and Courage. These challenges bring joy and an air of extreme satisfaction. The more difficult the challenge, the most satisfaction, excitement and exhilaration we feel.

4. **Skills can be improved through persistence**

   The SAM knows and believes that the need for improvement is a constant. Improvement requires persistence through trial and error, training, coaching and desire to learn. Those who do not understand the continuous skill improvement commitment are yielding to the misinformed concept that their skills are fixed.

I enjoy teaching and through this book I have enjoyed taking you on a new journey to sales success. You must not just learn how to sell products and services, but also learn to:

- Spend more time gathering the knowledge you need on becoming a better sales person

- Take more time to identify your shortcomings and to adopt the correct mindset to overcome these shortcomings

- Mold, shape and help yourself through the transition process and elevate yourself from being an average sales person to an exceptional salesperson

- See the distinction between the conventional sales philosophy and an exceptional SAM sales philosophy

A Final Comment

I am and will always be an "Outrageous" sales professional. I will always live my life and succeed as the Ultimate Sales Assassin Master. I hope that I have challenged the way you think, act, behave and challenge yourself in your every endeavor. The SAM **needs to be a smart and practical thinker** transforming yourself into a tenacious business improvement specialist. This is the challenge and attitude that you must take in your engagements with clients. Find your SAM DNA...Find Your Outrageous commitment to success... Become the Sales Assassin Master.

Final Wisdom from Anthony Caliendo,
the Ultimate Sales Assassin

We must get ready for tomorrow, today. That's what this book is all about. The Sales Assassin creates a long-term destination for your business and provides you a "Roadmap" for winning and achieving Sales Success.

ABOUT THE AUTHOR

We all know the business world changes around us with relentless speed and intensity. It takes great vision to not only see these changes, but more importantly to be able to anticipate and react with the tenacity to sustain success. There are few business leaders that possess the innate skills to maneuver the modern day challenges of today's business. Anthony Caliendo is one of these self-made men, an entrepreneur and corporate visionary. To thrive in business and beyond, professionals like Anthony have learned to look ahead, read and understand the trends and dynamic forces that will shape our business in the future and move swiftly to prepare for what's to come. Anthony is proud to be a professional salesman with super-sensory sales skills, proven success in sales strategy and corporate leadership, who has generated hundreds of millions in sales revenues and trained thousands of sales pros in various industries over the past 25 years to define him as the Ultimate Sales Assassin Master! At a very young age, he discovered his entrepreneurial instincts that serve as the basis for his desire for success, fortune and power. At 18, he became the youngest manager at that time to oversee Chicago Health Clubs and at 24 with his mentor, Al Philips, built the World Gyms with Arnold Schwarzenegger.

Never to miss a business opportunity, Caliendo found himself on Wall Street as a stock broker where his sales instincts and thirst for sales domination accelerated. This financial success on Wall Street to a number of notable business ventures, Caliendo mastered the art of personal branding when he became known as "The Main Man" in the mortgage business, architect of one of South

Florida's most successful conglomerate mortgage and real estate services and a local celebrity regularly featured on TV, radio and at special events. During the housing market crisis and the US's worst economic recession since the Great Depression, Caliendo re-invented himself and became the #1 Italian Cheese Salesman in the U.S., known as the iconic "The Big Cheese" and "The Cheese Boss." Caliendo directed his manufacturing plant's national and global expansion initiatives and doubled the company's revenues inside of 5 years. Caliendo defines himself as an "outrageous and relentless sales professional." With his outrageous and relentless mentality he constructed a fail-proof sales model encompassing specific skill sets and concepts that would be the foundation of sales training for his brokers, salespeople and the sales staffs of his clients. The concepts and motivational themes of past and present sales experience inspired him to write "The Sales Assassin" and become a sales motivational speaker and sales coach to salespeople in all industries. Caliendo lives, works and plays in south Florida with his wife, Lynette and their children: Shawyn, Steven, Kristen, Anthony, Jr., Giovanni, Gianna Bella, Isabella and Luciano.

For more information on motivational speaking, coaching services or for media opportunities please visit http://www.thesalesassassin.com or contact Anthony Caliendo at + 1-561-265-1405 or by email info@thesalesassassin.com

APPENDIX

THE 9 SALES ASSASSIN
MASTER BELTS

SAM Belt 1: Passion, Dedication, Courage

SAM Belt 2: Mental Preparedness Development

SAM Belt 3: Establishing the Sales Assassin Mindset

SAM Belt 4: Goal Setting and Achievement

SAM Belt 5: Client Qualification Process

SAM Belt 6: The Mastery of Leadership Integrity

SAM Belt 7: Reinvestment in Your Business and You

SAM Belt 8: Lessons of Life

SAM Belt 9: Lifestyle Change

HOW TO CONQUER YOUR SALES FEARS

Five common sales worries business owners face—and ways you can combat them to close the deal.
By Lisa Girard[45]

The expression, "He could sell ice to an Eskimo," acknowledges that certain people are born salespeople.

For most small-business owners, however, the selling process is anything but easy. In fact, when it comes to pitching their product or service, many entrepreneurs struggle with any number of issues, including lack of confidence in themselves or their product, fear of failure and fear of closing the deal. The good news: Experts say these fears can be overcome with the proper attitude, training and practice.

Here are five of the most common fears about selling and how they can be conquered.

***Fear No. 1: You will make a negative first impression.** We all know how important a first impression is, and the fear that you will not make a good one can be intense. It may even make you avoid meeting ideal prospects.*

***How to overcome it:** Show credibility through your appearance and nonverbal behavior, says Larina Kase, author of Clients, Clients and More Clients: Create an Endless Stream of New Business with the*

45   Girard, L. (2014). How to conquer your sales fears, http://www.entrepreneur.com/article/220691

Power of Psychology (McGraw-Hill, 2011). Research shows that people are attracted to others who dress like them, she says, adding, "If your audience is school-aged girls, you may wear hot pink or purple, or if your audience is conservative business suit types, you may wear a suit with a bright shirt or tie, something that also shows your personal style." Focus on nonverbal behaviors like smiling (though not a "perma-smile"), eye contact and open posture, and be sure not to fidget and play with keys or other objects.

***Fear No. 2: You will be rejected.** Experienced salespeople know they aren't going to be successful 100 percent of the time, but newcomers may regard failure as the end of the world. Joe Stewart, owner and general manager of Danco Transmission in Fairfield, Ohio, remembers attempting his first sale at age 21. "I almost turned white with fear from what might happen if they said that awful two-letter word we all despise as salespeople, 'No,'" he recalls.*

***How to overcome it:** Professionals not only know rejection happens, they look forward to it, says Peter Shallard, a Sydney, Australia-based business psychology expert and blogger. Understanding the reasons behind a rejection can help you refine your product and presentation. Stewart, now 43, reflects on that first experience, saying, "For me, the only way to beat that fear was to confront it. The more I did it the better I became at it, and less fear was the result."*

***Fear No. 3: You'll come across as pushy.** We've all had at least one negative experience with a salesperson who kept pushing and pressuring and wouldn't let us leave or hang up the phone. Many business owners worry they'll make prospects feel that way.*

***How to overcome it:** Kase suggests focusing more on having a conversation with someone than simply selling. Learn the prospect's* *needs and ask yourself if what you're offering is of real value to that person. When you care about your prospective customer and develop a sense of trust, you're more likely to make the sale. "My first customer let me know that at first they felt uncomfortable due to the horror stories they had heard about other auto repair places," Danco's Stewart says. "But that quickly subsided after speaking with me because I made them feel as though they were family."*

Fear No. 4: You won't deliver. *Even when you do get a yes, you may fear you won't be able to fulfill all of the person's expectations. You may even suffer from the "Impostor Syndrome," which means you're starting to question the value of your own products.*

How to overcome it: *Kase suggests gathering feedback from customers and taking note of all the ways you have delivered. That approach helped Christine Buffaloe, who started Serenity Virtual Assistant Services, an online business management service, in 2005, and feared people would think she wasn't worth what she was charging. Buffaloe says she gained confidence from reading the testimonials on her own website. "Continuously look for ways to improve your services so you are sure you're providing optimal value," she adds, "and you will always be confident in your abilities."*

Fear No. 5: You don't know if you're doing it right. *Going into sales without any training can be terrifying. How do you know you're using the right tactics and offering people what they need?*

How to overcome it: *Debra Condren, president and CEO of Manhattan Business Coaching and author of Ambition is Not A Dirty Word (Broadway, 2008), recommends learning sales techniques by attending a training program. When Tanner Shepard co-founded Austin, Texas-based Ranch Road Creative Solutions, a marketing services provider, in*

2005, he was thrust into a sales role and gained confidence only after an intensive weekly sales course. "I had to challenge myself out of my comfort zone," he says.

SAM DEVELOPMENTAL ASSESSMENT

Assessing Your Sales Assassin Competencies:

1. How do you view your performance against each of the Sales Assassin Belts?

   Scale: 5 = Superior, 4 = Above the Expected,
   3 = The Norm or The Expected, 2 = Below Expected,
   1 = People Question My Behavior

   a. SAM Belt 1: Passion, Dedication, Courage

   b. SAM Belt 2: Mental Preparedness Development

   c. SAM Belt 3: Establishing the Sales Assassin Mindset

   d. SAM Belt 4: Goal Setting and Achievement

   e. SAM Belt 5: Client Qualification Process

   f. SAM Belt 6: The Mastery of Leadership Integrity

   g. SAM Belt 7: Reinvestment in Your Business and You

   h. SAM Belt 8: Lessons of Life

   i. SAM Belt 9: Lifestyle Change

2. Whether you agree or disagree, what would your peers or contemporaries describe as the lowest point of your SAM competency?

3. Whether you agree or disagree, what would your peers or contemporaries describe as the greatest point of your SAM competency?

4. In our professional lifetime, we are each proud and not so

proud of things we have done in terms of our SAM journey. Be Specific:

What, When, Where, Why?

a. What are you proud of?

b. What would you like to have done differently?

c. How did others respond?

5. What is the gap between your SAM performance level today and your vision for the future?

a. SAM Belt 1: Passion, Dedication, Courage

b. SAM Belt 2: Mental Preparedness Development

c. SAM Belt 3: Establishing the Sales Assassin Mindset

d. SAM Belt 4: Goal Setting and Achievement

e. SAM Belt 5: Client Qualification Process

f. SAM Belt 6: The Mastery of Leadership Integrity

g. SAM Belt 7: Reinvestment in Your Business and You

h. SAM Belt 8: Lessons of Life

i. SAM Belt 9: Lifestyle Change

SALES ASSASSIN PERSONAL ASSESSMENT

Your Personal Values and Ethics

The most important elements of your Sales Assassin journey are values and moral principles. This exercise is an opportunity to document your moral compass. In this exercise, you are asked to identify and explore your values, ethics, and moral direction.

1. In your life and in your SAM journey, identify your values.

2. Where do you believe each of these values originated?

3. How are your values integrated into your SAM journey? How do you live your values in your professional life?

4. Are your clients able to discern and identify your values from the way you do business?

5. Which of your values is sacred and you refuse to compromise no matter what?

6. In your job, are you ever in the position when you are challenged to compromise your sacred values? How do you resolve your dilemma?

7. How do the 9 SAM Belts support your values positioning? Are there conflicts?

REMEMBERING WISDOM FROM ANTHONY CALIENDO, THE ULTIMATE SALES ASSASSIN

***

Your ability to maneuver within the chaos of a massive corporation requires the strength and willingness to at times fail before succeeding, but it also requires the corporation be willing to allow you to learn from your failures and for the corporation to realize that your failure is also the organization's failure.

***

The right mindset creates and paves the way to success. It motivates us and makes us more productive each day.

***

My watch only tells me the time of day. It does not control me. I tell myself when I want to get things done. I must control me. This is my mindset.

***

The Formula = Think Really Big, But Start Small, One Day At A Time, One Win At A Time

***

SAM exhilaration is the ability to achieve success by setting your goals high enough for satisfying achievement!

***

The ability to overcome failure is our ability to embrace the chance to learn—the challenge to demonstrate Passion, Dedication and Courage

***

Life Can Teach You Many Things, But You Have To Be Willing To Learn

***

I seldom find sales people who grew up and went to college seeing sales as their great career choice.

***

We must get ready for tomorrow, today. That's what this book is all about. The Sales Assassin creates a long-term destination for your business and provides you a "Roadmap" for winning and achieving Sales Success.

REMEMBERING WISDOM FROM THE GREAT LEADERS

You can have unbelievable intelligence, you can have connections, you can have opportunities fall out of the sky. But in the end, hard work is the true, enduring characteristic of successful people."
—Marsha Evans

***

"Enchantment is the purest form of sales. <u>Enchantment</u> is all about changing people's hearts, minds and actions because you provide them a vision or a way to do things better. The difference between enchantment and simple sales is that with enchantment you have the other person's best interests at heart, too."
—Guy Kawasaki

***

"We've all heard about people who've exploded beyond the limitations of their conditions to become examples of the unlimited power of the human spirit.

You and I can make our lives one of these legendary inspirations, as well, simply by having courage and the awareness that we can control whatever happens in our lives. Although we cannot always control the events in our lives, we can always control our response to them, and the actions we take as a result.

If there's anything you're not happy about—in your relationships, in your health, in your career—make a decision right now about how you're going to change it immediately."[46]
—Tony Robbins

46   Goodreads. https://www.goodreads.com/author/quotes/5627.Anthony_Robbins

***

"Salespeople today ARE the differentiator. That's why it's so critical for you to focus on becoming a valuable business asset to your customers."

—Jill Konrath

***

"Remember that failure is an event—not a person."

—Zig Ziglar

***

"Failure is the condiment that gives success its flavor."

—Truman Capote

***

"Success is the ability to go from failure to failure without losing your enthusiasm."

—Sir Winston Churchill

***

"If you can dream it, you can achieve it."

—Zig Ziglar

***

"Passion is one of the most powerful engines of success. When you do a thing, do it with all your might. Put your whole soul into it. Stamp it with your own personality. Be active, be energetic and faithful, and you will accomplish your objective. Nothing great was ever achieved without passion."

—Ralph Waldo Emerson

***

"Success is a state of mind. If you want success start thinking of yourself as a success."

—Dr. Joyce Brothers

***

"Do one thing every day that scares you."

—Eleanor Roosevelt

***

"Tough Times Never Last, But Tough People Do."

—Dr. Robert Schuller

***

"Never give up on what you really want to do. The person with big dreams is more powerful than one with all the facts."

—Albert Einstein

***

"The best revenge is massive success."

—Frank Sinatra

***

"If you don't drive your business you will be driven out of business."

—B.C. Forbes

***

"Build your own dreams or someone else will hire you to do theirs."

—Farrah Gray

***

"Things do not happen; things are made to happen."

—John F. Kennedy

***

"The way to get started is to quit talking and start doing."

—Walt Disney

***

"Excellence is not a skill, it's an attitude."

—Albert Einstein

***

"High expectations are the key to everything."

—Sam Walton

***

"Success is not to be measured by the position someone has reached in life-but the obstacles he has overcome while trying to succeed."

—Booker T. Washington

***

"Every choice you make has an end result."

—Zig Ziglar

***

"There is no elevator to success. You have to take the stairs."

—Zig Ziglar

"Change starts with you, but it doesn't start until you do."

—Zig Ziglar

***

"If you don't know where you are going you'll probably end up somewhere else."

—Zig Ziglar

***

"Innovation distinguishes between a leader and a follower."

—Steve Jobs

***

"It's fine to celebrate success, but it is more important to heed the lessons of failure."

—Bill Gates

***

"Life is not fair. Get used to it."

—Bill Gates

***

"In essence, if we want to direct our lives, we must take control of our consistent actions. It's not what we do once in a while that shapes our lives, but what we do consistently."

—Tony Robbins

***

"If you're thinking already, you might as well think big."

—Donald Trump

***

"It's very important that people aspire to be successful. The only way you can do it is if you look at somebody who is."

—Donald Trump

***

"Failure is not an option. Everyone has to succeed."

—Arnold Schwarzenegger

***

"Winners never quit and quitters never win."

—Vince Lombardi

***

"I am the Greatest. I said that even before I knew I was."

—Muhammad Ali

A SURVEY OF
SALES EFFECTIVENESS

Global Research on What Drives Sales Success
Conducted By Achieveglobal

There are any number of surveys in any industry that provide insight into the issues and circumstances that drive a broad-based understanding into professional success. Achieveglobal, renowned global consulting firm, has 50 years experience in the area of employee development in a variety of disciplines. The firm conducted a worldwide survey of more than one thousand sales professionals to gain in depth insight into the challenges faced by these professionals.

The performance of sales professionals participating in the study is a key variable for comparing the relationship between the selection of sales activities and organizational support. More specifically, we would expect that specific sales activities tend to be selected as important success factors by higher performing salespeople, while those not performing as well tend to focus on other activities.

We observed sales performance in two ways. The first involved creating an indicator of success based on three questions relating to the percent change in quota, change in deal size, and change in overall sales revenue. These three questions were combined to create an index of overall individual sales performance for the past year. High Performers represent those who have a combined score that falls in the top third of the combined scores from the three questions, while Medium Performers fall in the middle third and Low Performers in the lowest third. This provides a comparison of respondents to others who answered the survey rather than to an industry or market benchmark.

The second method for observing success was merely to compare those respondents reporting an increase of more than 10% in sales growth from the prior year with those reporting more than a 10% decline in sales revenue. Overall, there is a moderate relationship between sales performance and the priority of sales activities for certain phases of the sales process as measured by the performance indicator and change in sales revenue.

We would also expect that the performance of salespeople be related to organizational support, since organizational support should improve sales results. Again, as we show on the next page in table 2, there are relationships between performance and ratings of several selling-support activities.

- *High performers were more likely to select the following as being critical to their success:*
  - *Possess an understanding of products/services being sold.*
  - *Have an in-depth knowledge of the customer's industry.*
  - *Identify new opportunities in existing accounts.*
  - *Conduct in-depth research of prospect organizations.*
  - *Ensure that the organization delivers what is promised.*
  - *Exhibit sales tenacity.*
- *Lower performers more often selected the following as one of their top three success factors:*
  - *Actively build and maintain a network of contacts.*
  - *Aggressively pursue leads.*

> ➤ *Tell stories to illustrate important points.*

> ➤ *Look for innovative ways to meet client needs.*

> ➤ *Provide customers with ongoing advice.*[47]

---

47   AchieveGlobal. 8875 Hidden River Parkway, Suite 400, Tampa, Florida 33637 http://www. achieveglobal.com/resources/files/AG__SurveyofSalesEffectiveness.pdf

INDEX

Made in the USA
Middletown, DE
07 May 2017